Laughs & Lessons: Stories From an Insurance Career

by Larry Goanos

About the cover photo: Taken in December of 2022 at Perch, a restaurant in downtown Los Angeles, this photo features, from left, the author, Ryan Pincus and Brian Cardoza, a Southern California attorney and law school classmate of the author. That night, Ryan and Brian discussed with great zeal their mutual love of the sport of wrestling and the people they both knew. It was the last time the author would have the great pleasure of Ryan's company.

For the Pincus Family

CONTENTS

DEDICATION

This book is dedicated to the memory of my friend Ryan Pincus. He was an insurance executive, yes, but more importantly, he was an extraordinary person.

Ryan was energetic, fun, funny, intelligent, and generous. I didn't know Ryan nearly as well as many people did, but I know he was a beloved son, brother, uncle, colleague and friend to all who knew him. Ryan lived life to the fullest – until he tragically fell victim to gun violence at age 37 in August 2023 while on a business trip in San Francisco.

An entire book of interesting and funny stories could be written about Ryan's adventures in insurance, and life. Unfortunately, I don't know many of those stories, but I will share one that I do know. I related this tale to the 500-plus attendees at his memorial service in New Jersey in the summer of 2023, where I was one of 11 speakers. For as great an honor as it was to speak at Ryan's memorial service, a truly uplifting and inspiring event, I'm sure everyone present would have much preferred to have been dancing at his wedding.

After graduating from high school in Madison, N.J., where he was a star on the school's wrestling team, Ryan attended West Virginia University. His parents, Rene and Steve, helped move Ryan into his dorm on his first day at WVU. While unpacking the family car in Morgantown, Steve lifted Ryan's backpack from the trunk and noticed it was unusually heavy. Steve unzipped it and found a six-pack of beer nestled within. Underaged freshmen were not allowed to drink alcohol at WVU.

Steve said to Ryan, "What's with this six-pack?"

"Dad," Ryan said, "It was lying around at home, and I didn't want to see it go to waste, so I brought it along."

Steve's quick reply: "You know what I don't want to see go to waste? All the tuition money we're paying to send you here." With that, Steve removed the beers from the backpack and returned them to the car.

But hey, you can't blame a kid for trying!

We lost Ryan far too soon – a tragedy not just for his family, friends and the insurance industry, but for all who might have been fortunate enough to have met him in the past, or who would have met him in the future. Those of us lucky enough to have known Ryan will never let his memory fade. To insurance industry people, I say: Ryan was one of us; Ryan was the best of us.

In some cultures, there's a belief that by saying the name of a deceased loved one aloud, we perpetuate their memory and keep them alive in a way.

Dedication

I hope that *Laughs & Lessons: Stories From an Insurance Career*, all profits of which will be donated to the Ryan Pincus Memorial Fund, will be one small part of the enduring effort to say Ryan's name and to keep his memory alive.

The Ryan Pincus Memorial Fund is a fund created to provide college scholarships and other benefits to those in need. It has been modeled after the generous and supportive ways in which Ryan lived his life. Learn more at https://charitysmith.org/ryan-pincus-memorial-fund/

Ryan's childhood baseball card.

Author's BS Disclaimer (You knew there had to be one):
My memory isn't perfect, but I've made a sincere effort at
recounting the circumstances of each story, and each line of dialog,
as accurately as I could. In some instances, I had to take a bit of
literary license, but it was never my intent to change the overall
message, or tone, of any conversation. This book is meant as a
tribute to the commercial insurance industry and the people in it,
and nothing herein is intended to embarrass, belittle or criticize
anyone (a thinly disguised effort to preclude lawsuits against me, I
admit!) In my view, if you're mentioned in this book, it's a
compliment. You are one of the many people who have brightened
my personal insurance journey and have made it more memorable.

And, again, all the book's proceeds go to charity, so please keep
that in mind before voicing any complaints or filing any litigation.
Thank you!

FOREWORD

By Jon Reiner, President RT ProExec

Ryan Pincus was a dear friend of mine. We met in 2012 through the financial lines insurance industry, but from the day I met Ryan he felt like an old friend that I had grown up with.

Ryan and I shared many great memories ranging from fun dinners, boat rides and fitness classes, to baseball games with our fathers. Ryan and I had so many laughs together that it would be impossible to count them.

I cannot believe that I am writing the Foreword to a book dedicated to the memory of Ryan – and to benefit his Memorial Fund – after he has left us at such a young age, another tragic victim of senseless gun violence.

Ryan touched many lives deeply, mine included, during his too-short time on this Earth, but his memory will long endure.

This may be the Foreword to a book dedicated to Ryan's memory, but it won't be the Last-Word. Ryan's memory will live on in all of us who were privileged enough to have known him.

A Message from Ryan's Parents, Rene and Steve Pincus

Ryan Pincus is our son. On August 4, 2023, he was shot, murdered on the streets of San Francisco. That day started for him as a typical day in the life of any insurance professional. Meetings with colleagues and trading partners, a ballgame, dinner, drinks. Unfortunately, on his way to his hotel, he went down the wrong street at the wrong time. He ended up in a verbal altercation that turned physical. One gunshot and it was over. The coward that killed him and fled is still on the run as of this writing.

Anyone who knew Ryan knew how much fun he was. A friend to all. He treated the trainee the same way he treated the CEO. Always there to help a friend or a colleague and generous to a fault. We wish we knew the extent of all he did and the love for him before his demise. As parents, we knew him primarily through that lens. Hearing from others about their relationship with him has been one of the few blessings of this whole ordeal.

His death has made us a lot of things. It has made us more cautious and conscious of our surroundings. It has made us more angry that our world is not as safe as it once was, especially our cities. It has made us sad. We have a hole in our hearts that can never be filled. But it has also made us more appreciative. Appreciative of all the support we received from family and friends. Appreciative of the time we had with Ryan and what a great man he turned out to be. And an appreciation for how short our lives really are. That appreciation makes it all the more important to try to enrich our lives every day. But it should never take a tragedy like this to teach us that lesson.

Thank you, Larry, so much for dedicating this book to the memory of Ryan. You are a dear friend and a real mensch.

INTRODUCTION

I know, I know, most people don't think there are interesting or funny stories emanating from the insurance industry, let alone life lessons.

In some ways, I don't blame them.

The insurance industry is portrayed in popular culture, and perceived by most people in society, as staid and boring.

A book about insurance? ZZZZzzzzz... no thanks, many would say; I'll just take Sominex to lull me to sleep. In fact, rather than read an insurance book, most people would choose to down a cocktail of antifreeze and broken glass, with a chaser of a shot of cockroaches fresh out of the blender.

OK, I'll try not to be so gross from here on out.

Anyway, to those who think insurance is boring, I'd say, *"Not so fast, bucko."*

Those who believe that nothing fun or interesting ever happens in the Wonderful World of Insurance clearly do not inhabit the Wonderful World of Insurance. Just the fact that I came up with the name, "Wonderful World of Insurance" shows how fun it is!

The general populace thinks insurance jobs involve nothing more exciting than consulting actuarial tables, calculating premiums, generating quotes, issuing policies and – occasionally, paying claims. They think it's a snooze fest. **WELL, WAKE UP BECAUSE I'M HERE TO TELL YOU IT'S NOT!**

I apologize for yelling. My bad.

Insurance jobs probably rank lower than accounting or engineering on the federal government's Entertaining Careers Scale (www.ECS.gov). That's a Department of the Commerce-created and federally funded scale measuring the humor and fun level of various professions. If you're not familiar with it, that's because I just made it up. See, we're being creative and having fun in insurance already! Welcome to the Wonderful World of Insurance! It's like Disney World, but with more characters, better food and more adult beverages!

Speaking of which, at a cocktail party, most insurance people dread that inevitable question: "So, what do you do for a living?" It's difficult for an Insurance Person to put an entertaining or intriguing spin on their work. Not one that will be appreciated by the Average Joe, or Average Jane, anyway.

"I underwrite D&O Insurance policies," doesn't usually light up the face of the person who asked the question. You may even notice their head bob forward as they struggle to stay awake. That would be a good time for a sidestep to avoid having them nod off into your martini. It has happened.

However, most people's view of the insurance profession is highly inaccurate.

The insurance industry is teeming with interesting, unique and entertaining people and situations, but they simply don't get the publicity of, say, the Kardashians. Just by mentioning that family, sales of this book are projected to increase by at least 300 percent. In fact, to really juice sales, I should have titled the book, "Stories About Keeping Up with The Kardashians, The Real Housewives, Taylor Swift and The Insurance Market."

As you might have guessed by now, I'm not above that. Not by a longshot. I'll see what the publisher thinks about this title.

Writing this book was not as easy as I had expected. I had to scour my memory for wholesome(ish) stories that would not embarrass or denigrate anyone – except maybe me. Some of you may be asking, "Who is this guy to be writing a book of insurance industry stories?"

Good question.

In my opinion, I'm nobody special; I'm just one of many thousands of people in the commercial insurance industry. But I looked around and didn't see anyone else writing a book like this, one intended to show the lighter and more "fun" side of our industry. I solicited stories from my 4,500+ LinkedIn connections, multiple times, but I only received one response. It was from Steve Pincus, Ryan's dad, who sent his contribution about three months before Ryan's passing. Thus, all of the stories in this book, save for that one, are from my experiences.

It is my fervent hope that this book will be a useful tool to help attract young people into an insurance career (as well as to help retain some of the young folks in the early stages of an insurance journey).

I thought it was important to try to get some fun and interesting stories in front of young people who may be considering what they'd like to do with their lives. As noted, the insurance industry has a bad public image – especially in the minds of today's youth – and this book is an effort to counter that thinking.

I really believe that if more young people knew the truth about an insurance career – namely that it's interesting, fun, challenging and can be very lucrative – then we wouldn't be facing such stiff challenges in attracting new talent to insurance.

That was my original intent in writing this book, although Ryan's untimely passing, sadly, motivated me to also help preserve his memory.

Before concluding this section, I'd like to acknowledge, and sincerely thank, Lee F. Lerner for his truly excellent work editing this book. Lee, who I have known since we were 11 years old, used his considerable talents to make the final product much better than the original draft I provided to him. He's open to freelance editing opportunities, including business documents, presentations, etc. You can contact him at LeeLerner916@gmail.com.

In addition, I'd like to thank an up-and-coming writer, Cynthia Marie Fraser Hedemark, a student at NYU who provided valuable insights to make my writing less "old school." She will, no doubt, have great success with her own writing down the road.

I'd be remiss if I didn't also thank Patrick Wraight and his colleagues at Wells Media, publishers of this book (and two of my previous works.) They are top-notch professionals in every way, and if you're thinking of publishing an insurance book, I'd highly recommend that you talk to them.

OK, enough of the preamble. In these pages, I present you with what I believe to be some funny and interesting insurance stories from my career. I hope that they will enrich you in one way or another, whether it be by inducing laughter or prompting you to think about something in a new way.

I hope you will enjoy the read, and thanks again for supporting the Ryan Pincus Memorial Fund with your purchase. Many people, including me, appreciate your efforts.

CHAPTER 1: DON'T TAKE YOURSELF TOO SERIOUSLY

In the late 1990s, when I was working at a subsidiary of American International Group (AIG), my boss, Bob Omahne, was an innovative guy who was on the cutting edge of a product known as "Finite Risk Insurance." Bob had a background in accounting (snoozer...) before getting into insurance, and he knew a lot about the intricacies of tax laws and accounting standards, which made him an ideal Finite Risk salesman/underwriting manager.

Finite Risk was the marquee product of our AIG subsidiary in those days. Bob would close lucrative deals that resulted in hundreds of millions of dollars of gross written premium going to AIG's top line. Although, as he'd admit occasionally during moments of weakness, only a tiny portion of that eye-popping top-line number would "stick to our ribs" and result in actual revenue for AIG. For example, while we might book a $90 million in gross written premium deal, at the end of the day, AIG only would keep about $600,000 of that (hypothetical example here Bob – please don't call to correct me!)

I didn't fully understand how Finite Risk Insurance worked back in those days, and I still don't, but suffice it to say that the product was in the spotlight because of the huge numbers it would produce.

The revenue looked great on paper, and Bob was an insurance superstar. At least in our company.

Now to the story (it'll be worth it):

I was golfing with Bob and some insurance brokers in Bermuda in 1999 or so, when he received a call on the golf course from his assistant. She told Bob that a guy from The Wall Street Journal had called for him, and he left a number. Bob said to her, "Have Joe in the AIG Corporate Communications Department call the guy to pre-screen the questions. There's a lot going on right now with Finite Risk, and in insurance and finance in general, and I don't want to be caught off guard by a tough question. Hank [Greenberg; the then-AIG CEO] will not be happy with me if I say something wrong. I want to know the questions first so I can think about my answers."

Bob ended the call and returned to our golf game.

Over the course of the next half-hour or so, Bob said to anyone who would listen, "I may have to walk away to take a call from The Wall Street Journal. They're calling to interview me. I'll need quiet, so I'll just have to walk away from you guys. I just wanted to let you know in advance."

Basically, he was telling anyone within earshot that his work was important and high-profile enough that The Wall Street Journal wanted to interview him. Bob told at least four or five different groups of people about this impending Wall Street Journal call.

14

Eventually, Bob's assistant called back.

"Bob," she said, "Joe in Corporate Communications called the Wall Street Journal guy for you."

"Great, do you have the questions?"

Her response: "He wants you to know that your subscription is expiring next month."

Yes, really!

To his credit, Bob laughed, as did everyone else in the foursome. The lesson here: Being able to laugh at yourself is a humanizing trait and a valuable skill. And I think Bob renewed his subscription just in time.

PS Another note about Bob. When he was working (he's long retired now) he had a dry, under-the-radar sense of humor. It would pop up occasionally. One incident I remember clearly: He and I were walking through a parking lot after a meeting at Fannie Mae headquarters in suburban Washington, D.C., when he received a call on his cell phone telling him that the son of an AIG senior executive had just been hired into the company.

I asked, "Does he have a title?"

"Yeah," Bob deadpanned, "Next-of-kin."

CHAPTER 2: THE SWEATSHIRT

In the mid-1990s, my employer, AIG, was a major sponsor of the
U.S. Open Tennis Championships (Note: a torn rotator cuff
prevented me from qualifying in those days. Oh, yeah, and a lack
of tennis talent.) As a byproduct of this sponsorship, AIG had
access to some sweet courtside seats, an enclosed private spectator
box, and some excellent U.S. Open/AIG-logoed swag.

One year, AIG's New York Regional Vice President at the time,
Bob Parnell (a great guy; may he rest in peace) gave me some
primo U.S. Open tickets to entertain brokers and clients. On top of
that, and this was totally unnecessary and unexpected, he
interofficed me a very stylish white U.S. Open sweatshirt with the
AIG logo on it (I wish I still had it...)

Fast forward a few months.

Mr. Parnell sent a lovely and intelligent young woman (a William
& Mary grad) from his staff to interview with me for an
underwriting position with the Financial Institutions Group.
Judged by today's more politically correct and supportive
workplace standards, AIG's FI Group in the 1990s was the Wild
West of Insurance. Other parts of AIG were wild as well, but I
don't know their stories, although I do know that virtually every
division of the company in those days was very successful.

This woman, who shall remain nameless because she doesn't particularly care for this story (oh, and I don't want to get sued), came to my office on the second floor of 70 Pine Street to be interviewed. She sat in my office and maintained her composure, to her great credit, while three or four colleagues (I'm guessing it was John Rudolf, Neil Metzheiser, Rich Fernandez and Greg Bert) and I group-interviewed her. Questions were flying from every direction. And, all the while, the boys and I were tossing a Nerf football – when not shooting baskets at a small Nerf basket affixed to the back of my office door. (Note: Nerf products used to be an indispensable tool in underwriting commercial insurance.)

This woman, young and a recent college grad, seemed a bit intimidated by this band of underwriting loudmouths. Or, at the very least, she was put off by our buffoonery. Despite the fact that she answered our questions adeptly, I thought she was a bit too introverted to be a successful underwriter. An important part of the underwriting job is striking up relationships with insurance brokers, and clients, as well as coworkers. My impression, admittedly gleaned while multitasking in a manner that would befit Bart Simpson, was that she wouldn't be able to hack it. I thought the sharp edges and sharp elbows of AIG circa the late 1990s would prove too much for her.

So, I had a dilemma.

I didn't want to extend an offer, but Mr. Parnell had given me this great sweatshirt, and it would be an insult to him, professionally, if I didn't offer to hire his staffer.

After some deliberation, which involved weighing the prospect of making an enemy of Mr. Parnell – and losing access to a very cool swag-and-ticket pipeline – versus hiring a seemingly subpar underwriter, I did the only sensible thing, in my mind, and decided we should offer her a job.

Surprisingly, even after the Barnum & Bailey interview atmosphere, she accepted. The circus-like interview process hadn't soured her on the prospect of working in the F.I. Group. In retrospect, it's a good thing we hadn't deployed all of our elephants and monkeys during that interview!

And, as you might guess since this story is in the book, this woman turned out to be one of the best hires I ever made. Possibly the best ever. She stayed at AIG far longer than I did, and she would eventually go on to run a group of her own at the company. She was, and still is, a very talented, admired and intelligent insurance professional.

And she got her start in underwriting because of a sweatshirt.

A lesson I learned long ago, in part because of this incident: You can sometimes, but not always, judge a book by its cover. Interviews are not necessarily 100 percent indicative of whether a person will succeed, or not, in a job. Sometimes great interviewees fail at a job, and not-so-great interviewees reach the industry pinnacle.

It's a game of roulette (or Nerf basketball), and all you can do is give it your best shot. And hope to get a sweatshirt out of it.

End of lesson.

CHAPTER 3: NOT ALWAYS A HOLLYWOOD ENDING

In the early 2000s, when I was in the Financial Institutions underwriting group at AIG, I met with the board of Sovereign Bank (subsequently acquired by Santander Bank in 2010 if you're in the mood for some boring bank trivia) (and who isn't?) The entire board was at the meeting in a conference room at the bank's headquarters in Wyomissing, Pennsylvania. I was accompanied by two AIG colleagues and the insurance broker on the account.

We were attempting to convince Sovereign to move their Directors & Officers Liability (D&O) Insurance from CNA to AIG. This is always a challenge; it's like getting someone to stop drinking Coke and switch to Pepsi. Or, sometimes, it's akin to the even more difficult challenge of persuading them to switch to store-brand generic cola. When humans are comfortable with something, it's tough to get them to change.

Earlier, in 1994, Sovereign had acquired Shadow Lawn Savings and Loan, a bank headquartered near where I grew up at the Jersey Shore. My mother had helped me open my first bank account, a savings account, at Shadow Lawn when I was a kid. I still had the canceled savings account passbook.

Note to young people: In the olde days, when you opened a savings account at a bank, you received an actual booklet, called a "passbook," (roughly the size of a U.S. passport) in which the bank stamped a running tally of your account balance as you made deposits and withdrawals (perhaps to buy some store-brand generic cola!) When you closed the account, the bank would puncture holes through passbook to signify that it was now invalid.

In a theatrical effort to win the account, and employing my best thespian skills, I explained to the entire Sovereign board that I had been a customer of their now-subsidiary in my childhood, and I hoped they would reciprocate the trust that I had in them by moving their D&O insurance to AIG. (Note: Of course, as a 12-year-old, I didn't really have any genuine "trust" in their bank, I simply opened an account at the bank of my mother's choice. It could have just as easily been the Bank of The Cosa Nostra and I wouldn't have known the difference!)

At the conclusion of my seemingly heart-warming presentation (I didn't actually see any board members reaching for tissues, but I'm sure it happened; of course, they might also have been Bored Members), I reached into my suitcoat pocket and dramatically pulled out the canceled passbook and waved it around for all to see. This object of antiquity was proof of my former relationship with a bank acquired by Sovereign. It was, to me, a grand gesture worthy of a Hollywood blockbuster, akin to the last-second surprise revelation of important evidence in a tension-filled trial. Rousing applause and cheers filled the board room after I displayed the canceled Shadow Lawn passbook!

Well, maybe not, but that's how I remember it. I'm doing my best here folks.

I'll save you some time and cut to the climax: *We didn't get the business.*

It turned out that Sovereign had an open claim with CNA, and the bank didn't want to disrupt its relationship with their incumbent insurer by moving its coverage to AIG before the claim was fully resolved.

This is a valuable lesson from the insurance (and business) world: You don't always get the Hollywood ending. But keep trying kids, keep trying!

CHAPTER 4: THE BIG HEAD AT THE HEAD OF THE TABLE

Commercial insurance underwriters, especially those in professional lines insurance (which, generally speaking, is insurance that covers loss arising from the acts of professionals) frequently have leeway to adjust a premium amount before they quote it to an applicant. Pricing commercial insurance policies can be a somewhat fluid art depending upon a variety of factors. Sometimes, insurance people joke that we arrive at professional lines insurance premiums using dartboards and dice. That's not strictly true, but occasionally it's not too far off.

Underwriters, while making their calculations, can raise premiums by applying a "debit" to the premium calculation that is dictated by an underwriting formula, or, if appropriate, they can give an applicant a "credit" that will lower the premium.

The reasons as to why an underwriter would apply a debit or a credit to an account can vary greatly. Among the factors can be such things as the applicant's geographic location, the experience and talent level of its management team and the company's claims history. Of course, other factors affecting the premium quoted can come into play too, such as how annoying their insurance broker is ("close talkers" are among the worst) or what kind of offensive cologne the applicant's risk manager wears in abundance. Well maybe not those two factors exactly, but along those lines. You get the picture.

Below are two of my favorite examples of debits being applied to a formula-driven premium in order to increase the price based on factors not in said formula.

There is an unwritten rule in the commercial insurance industry – many of our rules are "unwritten" – that says if you invite someone to a business lunch, you are tacitly agreeing to pay for that lunch. I suspect this rule also applies in the larger business world beyond insurance, but it definitely applies in insurance.

Long ago, when I was at a large insurance company that shall remain nameless for the purposes of this story, an underwriter told his manager – we'll call the manager Mr. X – that an insured and their broker had invited the underwriter and Mr. X to lunch to discuss the upcoming policy renewal. It was a fairly large account, a big broker/dealer firm, and the expiring premium was in the $400,000 range.

The lunch, at an upscale Manhattan restaurant, went well enough. A lot of small talk was exchanged concerning the insured broker/dealer firm and its future prospects, and there was also conversation about the insurance market in general. In short, the lunch was a bit of a snoozefest.

But then, things took a turn.

After everyone was sated, glowing in the aftermath of a delicious meal, the bill came. It was dropped by the waiter in the middle of the table like a hot potato. Or, to use another analogy, like the proverbial turd in the punchbowl.

Tradition being tradition, and unwritten rules still being rules, the unwritten nature notwithstanding, Mr. X and his underwriter leaned back in their chairs and continued to make small talk while allowing the policyholder and his broker ample time and space to reach forward to pick up the check. After all, the lunch was the idea of the broker and insured and they had extended the invitation.

Mr. X and the underwriter, expecting their hosts to pick up the check, waited.

And waited.

And waited.

And waited.

And waited.

And waited.

You get the picture by now; it was a loooooooong wait. A Mexican standoff (if we're still allowed to say that; if not, we'll just say a "Nationality-Neutral Standoff").

Eventually, it became painfully clear that the policyholder and the insurance broker were not going to pay the bill. Finally, the underwriting manager, Mr. X, brushed off the cobwebs on the check folio and inserted his corporate credit card. An unwritten rule had been broken, and there would be repercussions!

About two weeks later, the underwriter entered Mr. X's office to review the quote for the Short-Armed Policyholder who failed to pay the lunch bill. The underwriter had to get Mr. X's approval to release the quote because it was outside of his underwriting authority. The underwriter explained his thought process on the account, citing a number of relevant considerations. The insurance company's established underwriting rating plan produced a quote of $410,000 for the renewal policy.

Mr. X was about to provide his approval of this quote when he remembered something.

"Hold on a second," he said to the underwriter.

He then opened his desk drawer and rifled through his expense statements. He found the bill for the offending lunch. "That quote is fine but add $422.65 to it. That's the cost of our lunch." The underwriter did as he was told, and the policyholder wound up paying the full amount of the renewal quote, oblivious to the fact that the lunch bill had come back to them after all!

You won't see, "Failed to pay for lunch," in any insurance company's rating plan, but sometimes it's there between the lines, in the column that tallies unwritten rules. Indeed, there is no such thing as a free lunch.

Hopefully this leaves you hungry for another premium calculation debit story.

This one involves a New York state-based savings bank and a meeting that occurred in the 1990s. The underwriter in question, Bill Brennan, a naturally surly type (he'll read this book and will probably agree with that assessment; plus, he's retired, so nobody cares what he thinks anyway!), attended a meeting of the bank's entire board of directors to discuss their insurance program with them. This was during one of the fleeting "hard markets" in the insurance industry. A "hard market" is when insurance companies generally hold the upper hand; they can raise prices and tighten coverage terms at their discretion. But, of course, within reason. Bill sat patiently among the board members at a large conference room table awaiting the arrival of the bank's CEO. The designated starting time for the meeting came ... and went. Finally, the CEO showed, barreling into the conference room about 20 minutes late.

"I saved the seat at the head of the table for you," said Bob, one of the bank's obsequious directors, trying to curry favor with the CEO. Without missing a beat, the CEO replied, "Wherever I sit is the head of the table."

Boom! Mic drop.

Right then, Bill said he decided to add $10,000 to the quoted premium just because of the CEO's unmitigated arrogance. And, of course, the bank and its insurance broker never knew that they had paid an Arrogance Surcharge. Only in insurance folks, only in insurance!

Chapter 5: The Toothpick Trick

Although outsiders might not believe it, there are a lot of little quirky and fun incidents in the insurance industry. Or, if not "a lot," some anyway.

In this story, I will shield the identity of the insured company, but it is a 100 percent true story, just like all of the others in this book. Well, maybe some are only 98.5 percent true, let me get my slide rule and *pro rata* wheel to confirm that (if that line is funny at all, it would only be so to insurance geeks.).

When I was at ACE Insurance Company, in about 2003, an underwriter and I had lunch at a swanky Manhattan restaurant (the Manhattan in New York, not the one in Kansas) with the CFO of a company that operates a national chain of retail stores. The CFO was a nice enough guy, and we had an enjoyable lunch. His company's primary Directors & Officers ("D&O") Insurance policy was written by Chubb, and we were trying to steal it away (coincidentally, ACE and Chubb are now the same company). I still remember the numbers on the account, as any good insurance professional would. It was a primary $10 million limit of liability D&O Insurance policy for a premium of $600,000.

And we wanted it. Badly.

The insured company was well-run, the stock was performing admirably, and it appeared to be a great account to have from an insurer's perspective. And it probably still is (it continues to exist).

I'm something of an amateur magician – emphasis on "amateur" (although I have invented some of my own tricks, but that's for another book) – and I had one trick I was particularly fond of at this time that I wanted to show the CFO. It is called the "Toothpick Trick."

I'm about to impart to you some information that, in itself, is worth the cost of this book. Yes, just these few paragraphs will be worth the cost of the book, so PAY ATTENTION!

This trick only works at higher-end restaurants that have cloth napkins. It won't work at McDonald's. Or even Five Guys. And the cloth napkin has to have a seam going all the way around it.

The preparation for the trick starts when you enter the restaurant. You begin by surreptitiously grabbing two regular toothpicks. Many restaurants have toothpicks at the maître 'd stand when you first walk in (I'll pause while you marvel at my accurate spelling and punctuation of maître 'd; hey, it's not that easy!). Other restaurants have toothpicks at the bar. If this is the case, a few minutes after we all sit down at our table, I'll excuse myself to purportedly go to the men's room, but I'll make a detour to the bar area to snag two toothpicks.

Next, you covertly take one of the toothpicks into your hand and while people are talking at the table and not paying attention to you, you secretly twist the toothpick into one of the ends of the seam of the napkin. If you squeeze the end of the seam, it almost always opens enough for you to twist a toothpick into it. You should push/twist the toothpick into the seam until it's about an inch from the corner of the napkin. It won't be visible at this point since it will be totally enclosed within the seam. Once this is set up, you're ready to go.

"I have a trick for you, the best trick you'll ever see while seated at a table," is how I usually introduce the trick. Then I laid the cloth napkin flat on the table. Next, I produce the other toothpick from my shirt or jacket pocket and announce, "This is an ordinary toothpick that I got from the maître 'd stand when we entered; there's nothing special or unusual about it."

Then I lay the toothpick just off center on the napkin which is lying on the table. Next, I fold one of the corners of the napkin over the toothpick. Then a second corner is folded over the toothpick. The third corner that I fold over is the one with the decoy toothpick hidden in the seam. And then I fold the fourth corner over.

In my mind's eye, I remember exactly where the toothpick in the seam is. I spin the napkin around on the table once or twice, slowly, to throw everyone off so they don't remember exactly where the toothpick that I displayed was placed. I then grab the toothpick that is in the seam through the napkin and ask someone at the table to snap it while I hold it within the napkin. After that, you can have a second person snap it also if you'd like. Having a second person snap the toothpick adds to the theatrical flair (the bar for "theatrical flair" at insurance meals is pretty low, as you can see).

Next, I say, "The toothpick is undoubtedly broken, you felt it snap between your fingers, and you may have heard it too, correct?" The people who did the snapping will always agree.

Then you place the napkin back on the table and slowly unfold it, corner by corner, to reveal an unbroken toothpick in the center of the napkin. You then pick up the napkin and shake it to show everyone that there was no other toothpick hidden anywhere. Of course, in reality there was, but it's so well-hidden in the seam that nobody will detect it. I've done this trick at least 100 times, and I've never had anyone detect the hidden toothpick in the seam.

My explanation might not be crystal clear, but you can Google "Toothpick Trick," (Unfortunately, Google and YouTube have taken some of the mystery and fun out of a lot of things, including magic tricks) and see a video of exactly how to do it. Normally, I don't give away the secrets to my tricks, but this is an exception since you bought this very valuable book, so consider yourself special!

After I did the trick for the CFO of the retail chain, he was amazed. Everyone always is. He asked me how I did it, but I wouldn't tell him. I said, "If you give us your account, I'll tell you how I did it."

Two weeks later, the broker, who worked at Marsh in Richmond, Virginia, called me to say, "They're moving their primary D&O policy to ACE, but you have to call the CFO to tell him how you did that trick." Thus, thanks at least in part to the Toothpick Trick, we landed a $600,000 account.

Ever since that day, whenever I do the Toothpick Trick, I tell the audience, "This is a $600,000 trick, that's how much one guy paid to learn it!" And that statement is true, sort of. Anyway, you are now armed with the knowledge of the Toothpick Trick, use it for the greater good of mankind, my friends, and don't sell its secret to anyone for less than $600,000!

Oh, and if you do sell it for that much or more, please buy some more books; all the profits go to a great cause!

CHAPTER 6: LAPEL PINS

This story isn't funny, although you may think that none of the stories in this book are, but it's another lesson involving, and an illustration of, a simple point: Be careful of what you say.

When I was at AIG in the late 1990s and early 2000s, I noticed an interesting phenomenon. Whenever I visited a company in the Midwest, it seemed that a lot of employees wore lapel pins of their company's logo. Note: This is back in the day when men wore suits and ties to work. But on the coasts, people didn't seem to wear lapel pins nearly as much. Maybe the people on the coasts thought they were too cool for lapel pins (with one exception that I'll explain shortly). Another explanation I came up with was that people in the Midwest are just generally nicer than those on the coasts, and they were earnest in their loyalty to their employer, so they wore lapel pins to display their company pride.

From an insurance liability perspective, I felt that loyal employees were less likely to sue their employer for employment practices issues, therefore they wouldn't be triggering a claim under our Employment Practices Liability Insurance. Thus, it was my belief that generally, companies with a lot of loyal lapel-pin-wearing employees were better insurance risks. Granted, this was only my own homespun (some might say, "wacky") theory, but I went with it. My personal philosophy is that professional lines insurance underwriting is both an art and a science.

I made the mistake of telling my theory about Midwesterners and lapel pins to a risk manager in Iowa during a visit to his office one day. One thing I didn't realize at the time is that risk managers are generally a tightly-knit group within each geographic area – and sometimes nationally – and they talk to each other regularly about brokers, carriers, insurance products and other things related to insurance.

About six months after my discussion with the Iowa risk manager, we had decided to non-renew an account in Minnesota because it was facing some serious financial difficulties. Non-renewing an account was a rarity at AIG back in those days; we usually found a creative way to write a tough risk, so you know there were some significant problems with this particular company that we were non-renewing. I can't remember exactly what they were, but I'm sure they were formidable in our view. I remember the company's name, and it's surprisingly still around, but I'll withhold that information (again, trying to avoid lawsuits here people!)

The risk manager of this troubled Minnesota company demanded to have a conference call with the underwriter and his manager and his manager's boss (who was me). Things got a bit contentious during the call, mostly because the risk manager wouldn't accept our rationale for non-renewing his company's D&O Insurance.

Finally, near the end of the call he blurted out, "You should come to our office, all our employees are wearing lapel pins!"

Touché.

He had obviously talked to the Iowa risk manager and thought he could play on my seeming affinity for companies with employees who wore lapel pins. I was annoyed, and amused, by his attempt to change our mind about the non-renewal, but, nonetheless, we held firm.

The exception to my homespun rule about people on the coasts generally not wearing lapel pins came in the form of big international insurance brokerage Willis. In the early 2000s, their then-CEO was a big fan of employees wearing Willis lapel pins on their work attire, men and women. My understanding is that it wasn't officially required, but it was highly encouraged.

I heard a story that one morning a Willis client executive was running late for a meeting, and when he rushed into the firm's main reception area at the New York headquarters, he was surprised to encounter the lapel-pin-loving CEO standing in front of him. The CEO looked at him and said sternly, "Where's your lapel pin?!"

Without skipping a beat, the client executive looked down at his suit jacket, devoid of a lapel pin, and said, "Oh no, I left it on my pajamas."

The CEO reportedly laughed, and the client executive got away without a reprimand, but everyone in the company knew that this particular excuse could not be used with the CEO again. Another stellar example of creativity in the insurance industry: Don't sleep on how a sense of humor can sometimes get you out of a jam.

CHAPTER 7: INSURANCE GUY AS ROCK STAR

I'm happy to reveal the names of some of the companies involved in stories recounted in this book, but there are others who I need to shield. This story involves one of those protected entities. I will tell you that Company XYZ is one of the largest privately held companies in America, and its name is widely recognized nationally, and even internationally. Sorry for the tease, but, again, I'm trying to avoid lawsuits; it's a hobby of mine.

I'll dispense with the boring parts (or, at least the <u>more</u> boring parts) of this story and will tell you simply that when I was at AIG, my colleagues Bob Omahne and Susan Rivera were the architects of a large and complex insurance program that provided coverage for virtually every aspect of Company XYZ's business. I was not involved in the technical work of putting together the insurance program, I was just the (self-anointed) pretty boy spokesmodel for AIG. OK, OK, maybe not even that.

Let's just say I was acting as a client-relations guy. That's a fair description.

About six months after this massive insurance program was put in place, involving many millions of dollars in premiums, Company XYZ had its annual shareholders' meeting, which was open only to employees, since they were the only ones allowed to hold shares.

XYZ's risk manager invited me to go to a post-meeting party thrown by her boss, XYZ's treasurer. The party was held in the ballroom of the hotel where the annual meeting took place. XYZ Corporation also happened to own the hotel. I'm throwing that out there as a clue for you amateur insurance sleuths. [Note: I realize that there are no "amateur insurance sleuths," but I'm humoring myself after having grown up watching shows like "Columbo" and "The Rockford Files."]

I waited patiently in the ballroom, and shortly after the meeting let out, the room began to fill with shareholder employees. A few minutes into it, the assistant risk manager escorted XYZ's treasurer over to meet me. "This is the guy from AIG," he said. The treasurer smiled widely and said that he was very happy to meet me. He pumped my hand with the enthusiasm of a teenage girl meeting Taylor Swift. I was perplexed, to say the least. This was not the standard greeting that an insurance underwriter would receive, but, OK, whatever.

A few minutes later, another assistant risk manager brought the company's CFO over to meet me. The CFO, in case you don't know, is a BIG DEAL at pretty much any company. "This is the AIG guy," she said. The CFO also pumped my hand and greeted me like an old army buddy at a reunion. I was even more perplexed.

This little ritual continued with about three or four more senior executives of XYZ who were escorted over to meet me, The AIG

Guy. Each showed almost unbridled glee in meeting me and shaking my hand. I was confused and confounded.

Finally, after the parade of executives slowed, I asked one of the assistant risk managers, "Why are these people so happy to meet me? I'm just an insurance guy. They act like they're meeting Mick Jagger."

"Well," he said, "At the beginning of every year a bunch of senior executives get into a room and value the stock for internal purposes. As you know, only employees can be shareholders. Let's say theoretically that the CFO says, 'OK, we're starting off at $1,000 per share, then we have to deduct for potential liabilities.' This year, every time someone would raise a potential liability, like a big flood that could wipe out an office, or a costly employment-practices lawsuit, the risk manager would say, 'No, that's covered by the AIG insurance program, no need to take a deduction from the stock price.' So, in essence, the AIG insurance program is putting money into the pockets of the senior executives – and all employees. That's why you're a rock star around here."

I was flabbergasted, but also pleased. It was one of the few times that an insurance underwriter was the star of the show in a room full of C-Suite executives!

Chapter 8: The Greatest Risk Is Not Taking One

I started a weekly event to promote camaraderie among the troops when I worked at AIG in New York City. It provided a bit of fun at the end of a typically long and grueling work week. This morale booster came in the form of a putting contest that I'd conduct in the hallway at about 4 p.m. each Friday. Every participant would contribute $1 toward the pot, and it was winner-take-all. Our motto, coined by our colleague Brad Cushman, a great guy, but one of the cheapest human beings you'll ever meet (he will consider that statement to be a compliment!), was "One putt, no tears."

The objective was to make a putt into a metallic golf "hole" from a distance of about 20 feet or so. If nobody made the putt into the hole, the person whose ball came to rest closest to the hole would win the pot. And if two or more people made the putt, then there would be a putt-off, and they'd each get another shot and the ball that landed closest to the hole would win.

These putting contests were not only morale builders, but they also, in my opinion, fostered camaraderie among our colleagues. It really was like playing an abbreviated version of miniature golf, and everyone was able to participate, you didn't need to be a particularly skilled golfer to play, or win.

Shortly after 9-11, when we were allowed back into our downtown NYC offices at AIG, I conducted a "Screw the Terrorists" putting contest and we donated the entire pot to one of the 9-11 relief funds (AIG as a company had given $10 million). Granted, it was a small gesture, but it made us feel like we were doing something to support America and to provide comfort to the victims and their families.

Fast forward to the last Friday that I would work at AIG, in April of 2002. I conducted the most popular One Putt Contest of my career (which, granted, isn't really saying much). It was truly happenstance that about 30 people signed up, and I had decided to charge $10 per entrant, knowing that I would be leaving the company soon and this was my One-Putt Swan Song. But nobody else knew that at the time. The pot totaled an eye-popping $300, winner-take-all. This was the major leagues of insurance One Putt Contests!

I was in the Financial Institutions Group, which at that time was based on the fourth floor of 175 Water Street in downtown Manhattan. There was a stairway on our floor that led up to the Commercial D&O Group's offices on the fifth floor. I decided to hold the One Putt Contest in the hallway at the base of the stairway so people could line the stairway for optimum viewing pleasure. And what a pleasure it was. It was like something out of a movie, with 30 spectator/participants in the fourth-floor hallway area and all along the staircase leading up to the fifth floor. Standing room only, folks, you're lucky to be here! There were no ticket scalpers, but it felt like there should have been. To increase the dramatic effect, I set up the "course" as an extra-long 25-foot putt.

It takes a bit of time to get 30 people to each putt a golf ball. Believe it or not, before taking their putt, some people stretch, take practice swings, line up the putt, check the floor for irregularities, etc. But we got through it eventually.

After the first round, two people made the extra-long 25-foot putt. One was Tom McArdle, and the other was Matt Sweesy. Both are still in the insurance industry as of this writing and, not surprisingly, not on the PGA Tour. They were a bit of opposites as underwriters went. McArdle was a former high school athlete and kind of loud and boisterous. Sweesy, on the other hand, was a military veteran, and embodied the quiet and introspective type.

I said to each of them at the conclusion of the round, after they had tied, "We have a $300 pot, you can either split it so that you each take home $150, or we can have a putt-off and whoever makes it, or leaves their ball closest to the hole, wins the entire $300. What do you want to do?"

McArdle, the more outwardly aggressive of the two, immediately piped up. "Let's do the putt off, winner take all. I'm down for that."

Sweesy, in his reserved and gentlemanly manner, agreed, although a bit reluctantly in my estimation.

Most of the 30 participants had stuck around to see who would win. The stairway leading up to the fifth floor was still packed with spectators. The tension in the air was palpable. Only an ESPN camera crew was missing.

Some months earlier, I had removed an AIG logo from a baseball cap and my then-assistant, Rose Mosca, was nice enough to sew it onto the breast pocket of an old green plaid sportscoat I had purchased at a thrift store. This was our AIG F.I. Group's version of the legendary green Master's Jacket. Each week, the winner of the One Putt Contest would receive the jacket in a short, half-assed ceremony, and they would be allowed to keep it in their cubicle or office until the following week. So, in addition to the $300 cash, the right to wear the AIG Masters jacket was on the line. You, dear reader, are probably breaking out in a sweat just reading this.

Knowing that I'd be leaving the company the next week, I figured that whoever won the jacket this time would probably be keeping it forever. Talk about high stakes!

McArdle went first. He stretched his arms theatrically, spun his head around a bit to loosen his neck muscles, and generally made an exaggerated, theatrical showing of preparing to putt. The crowd was hushed. And riveted. McArdle brought the putter back slowly and hit the ball solidly. It looked like a good putt coming off the club face. It rolled along the carpeted hallway at a respectable pace, before coming to rest about 8 inches short of the hole. An impressive effort. McArdle was clearly pleased with himself as he surveyed the stellar result.

With his work cut out for him, Sweesy stepped up to the tee box-like area of the carpeted hallway. He took a deep breath and exhaled slowly. Actually, I don't remember if it was a deep breath or not, but I'm taking poetic license here to embellish the story like a Hollywood screenwriter. Or a John Street screenwriter. I'm sure that there's a good chance that Hollywood will option this book to make the first great insurance industry film (anyone have Tarantino's number?)

Sweesy looked around at the expectant crowd. Everyone wanted to see if he had it in him to beat McArdle's impressive effort. It would take an exceptional putt to win the $300 pot.

Sweesy pulled back the putter and struck the ball with a thud. It rolled down the carpeted hallway floor and kept rolling...and rolling...and rolling...and rolling...and rolling...and rolling...and rolling...and rolling...and rolling...and rolling...and rolling...and rolling...and rolling...until, finally, it began to slow as it approached McArdle's ball.

Would Sweesy's effort have enough juice to pass McArdle's ball and win the contest?

It drew even with McArdle's ball and then ... rolled a bit forward just ... another ... two ... inches. It was, just barely, the winner!

Matt Sweesy, an unlikely champion, had won the contest and its $300 prize, as well as the prestigious green thrift-store AIG logoed jacket that went with it.

The crowd went nuts!

When I went to my office to retrieve the $300 to pay Sweesy his winnings, and to get the jacket, I felt like McArdle should get something, also, for his second-place finish. I didn't have anything in particular in mind, but then, rooting around in my drawer, I found just the thing.

I went back to the hallway where 15 or so people were still lingering, and I made a big show of presenting the money and the jacket to Sweesy. Photos were taken and there were smiles all around.

Then I reached into my pocket and loudly proclaimed, "And Tom, you get this coveted prize for finishing second in this prestigious tournament. It's not $300, but it's something of great value... this AIG nail clipper."

Yes, really.

I gave McArdle a blue nail clipper with an AIG logo on it. He could have simply settled for $150 by splitting the pot, but as AIG used to say in one of its advertising campaigns long ago, "The greatest risk is not taking one." McArdle admirably (I guess?) took a bold risk and was rewarded with a nail clipper.

When I contacted him about this story before I wrote it for this book, Tom McArdle proudly noted that he still has the nail clipper. I'm not sure if Matt Sweesy still has the jacket, but I hope he does. And I hope he wears it occasionally as an homage to the old AIG F.I. Group.

Anyway, talk about your nail-biting competitions!

CHAPTER 9: SNAP DECISION

Many years ago (a fitting opening for most of the stories in this book...), I was at an insurance conference in Las Vegas with a bunch of colleagues. Among them were Vince McGeehan, my then-co-worker at ACE (now Chubb), along with Steve Sanford and Mark Borkovec, two Aon insurance brokers at the time.

[**Footnote Not Down in the Traditional Footnote Location**: Sadly, for me, all three of them are enjoying fabulous retirements as of this writing, while I'm still toiling away in the Insurance World!]

We had a free day before the conference started – "free days" and "insurance conferences" go together like peanut butter and jelly – and we decided to go golfing at one of the many Las Vegas courses.

It was a beautiful sunny Vegas day with low humidity, but poor Vince was having a bad day on the course. He's normally a pretty good golfer, but on this day, he just didn't have it. His shots, particularly his drives, were scattering everywhere, like cockroaches when you turn on the light in a New York City apartment. Vince's frustration finally reached a boiling point on the 14th hole.

He hit a drive that sliced far to the right. Picture in your mind MAGA right and then go even farther. That's pretty far right. The ball was obviously sick of Las Vegas and was making a break for Utah, or California. I'm not that good with directions. Wherever it headed, it was epic. In fact, people will probably write about that sliced golf drive in books someday. Oh, wait, someone is doing it now!

Being fed up with his game at this point, Vince lifted his driver high above his head and tomahawked it into the ground. The motion was like someone trying to ring the bell at one of those carnival attractions with a rubber sledgehammer. Those games purport to test how strong a person is. Vince would have easily rung the bell with his downward smash. In fact, I wouldn't be surprised if Vince's high-energy slamming of the golf club knocked a guy off his barstool down in China.

Vince's large, and expensive, golf club head snapped off the end of the shaft and flew about 6 feet away. With steam coming from his ears, Vince walked over, picked up the severed head (a New York Post headline in the making) and violently threw it into a nearby metal trash can. He then realized that the broken golf club shaft was still in his other hand, so he thrust the rest of the broken club into the same can, like a fencer jabbing at a hated rival. Vince had neatly disposed of all evidence of his disastrous drive. Or so he thought. Oh, and needless to say (but I'll say it anyway, just to rub it in), Vince didn't bother looking for the errant drive. It was probably rolling somewhere along Interstate 15 in Barstow, California.

What happened next is the reason there is a story at all to tell here, and full credit for that goes to Mark. As I got into the driver's seat of our golf cart and prepared to pull away, Mark said, "Whoa, wait, you're not going to just leave that club head in the garbage, are you? You should fish it out and use it for something in the future, some kind of practical joke on Vince."

Bingo! Mark didn't have to ask twice. A light, albeit a dark and evil one, went on in my head, and I did exactly as Mark suggested. I fished the broken driver head out of the trash and hid it in my golf bag. Vince and Steve had pulled away 20 seconds earlier, so they were not around to see this diabolical maneuver.

When I returned to New York after the conference, I found a trophy shop a few blocks away from our downtown offices. I had the place make a custom plaque using the snapped-off clubhead as the centerpiece. I asked them to surround the broken club head with green felt, approximating the grass on a golf course, and to inscribe it with the words, "The Vince McGeehan Don't Lose Your Head Award." Not the cleverest of puns, I'll admit, but it was the best I could do at the time.

When the customized plaque was ready, I set the full plan in motion. I decided I would call a meeting of all our underwriters, including Vince, who had some other non-underwriter title (the insurance industry is chock full of BS titles and they're hard to keep straight), and then I'd have Steve and Mark make a surprise entrance to award Vince this plaque.

I found out when Denver-based Steve and Mark would be visiting NYC for work, and I filled them in on my devious plan. They were, as expected, enthusiastically on board. (Note: I've played worse practical jokes in my life. For example, I once made two coworkers at my summer job driving a 7-Up truck believe they'd won $11 million in the New Jersey Lottery. They were fooled for about two minutes, during which time they went wild celebrating. They threw a bunch of 2-liter bottles of soda around a warehouse and yelled about how they were quitting ... until another coworker told them it was a practical joke that I had played on them. I know, it's hard to believe I lived to talk about it!)

The plan was for Steve and Mark to show up at our offices during the fake staff meeting – I was sure I could come up with some fictitious reason for a meeting that sounded legit enough to keep the group occupied until Steve and Mark arrived – and then they'd walk into the conference room to present Vince's plaque to him in front of everyone.

We set a date for the meeting, and the plan was put into motion. On that morning, I called an impromptu staff meeting with about 14 underwriters in one of our conference rooms at 140 Broadway in Lower Manhattan. However, there was a glitch. Steve and Mark had arrived in our offices about 20 minutes earlier than expected (probably my fault in not getting the schedule straight). They were seated in our main waiting area when Vince and the underwriters came walking down the hall past the reception area on their way to the conference room.

Vince saw Steve and Mark, two of his best friends in the insurance industry, and was crestfallen to discover that they were in our offices and had not called him in advance to plan a time to meet. When Vince asked them what they were doing in our offices, they said they had a meeting with the head of our group, Tim O'Donnell. Vince was majorly bummed. His good friends had seemingly overlooked him. And on a Friday no less.

A few minutes later, once our group was assembled in the conference room, Steve and Mark came in with the Vince McGeehan "Don't Lose Your Head" plaque. It got some laughs, but not as many as I'd expected. I explained the story behind the plaque to all the underwriters and reminded them that we needed to maintain our composure at work, then we adjourned the meeting. Steve and Mark hung out with Vince briefly, but as I recall, they had to get to a meeting at their employer's NYC office.

On the following Monday, I asked Vince what he thought of my little practical joke. His answer surprised me: "I thought the plaque was funny, I didn't mind it, but what really upset me was that two of my best friends in the insurance industry would come to our offices without calling me in advance. When I walked past the reception area and saw them sitting there, my heart sank, I was so disappointed that they hadn't called me. That's what really upset me!"

Ha. I guess you never know. Even the best laid plans of mice and men, as they say.

But at least I managed to surprise, annoy and razz him in some way, I consider that a win!

CHAPTER 10: HIGHWAY TO HELL, OR AT LEAST THE HAMPTONS

I wish I had a better title for this chapter, but that's the best I can do. I am striving mightily to keep some (but not necessarily all) of these stories sanitized so I don't end up on the wrong end of a defamation lawsuit. I hope you understand. To make it clear, I think it's worth repeating: **Please don't sue me people, this book benefits charity!**

I've worked for a few large companies during my insurance career, and I'm hoping you won't dissect my LinkedIn profile to figure out which one was involved in this story.

Anyway, a senior executive at a large company I worked for in the past agreed to drop into a meeting that one of his subordinates, a client-relations executive, was conducting with the CEO of one of the company's largest clients.

This pompous senior executive (we'll call him "Mr. Pompous") made it clear to the client-relations executive that he could only stop briefly to say hello to the client company's CEO (we'll call him "Client CEO"). Mr. Pompous made it clear to the client-relations executive that he was granting a significant favor to the client by stopping by to say a quick hello.

The client company was a manufacturer of a lot of technical machinery and equipment, things like helicopters, elevators and jet engines (that may give away the client company's identity; if you got it without Googling, kudos to you, you're the type of intelligent person I want reading my books!)

The Client CEO was a very wealthy and refined gentleman, and the meeting got off to a great start, I was told. Then, about 20 minutes into it, Mr. Pompous deigned to stop by for a few minutes to give the Client CEO the honour (intentionally sophisticated British spelling there) of a visit.

The talk somehow turned to the Hamptons, the Eastern Long Island beach playground of the rich and famous, and the Client CEO mentioned that he had a home there.

"Oh, then you must know my family's business," Mr. Pompous said, "It's right there on the Montauk Highway, you can't miss it, there's a big sign with our family name on it."

The Client CEO said that no, he wasn't familiar with the business or the family name.

Mr. Pompous was having none of this. He knew for a fact that everyone who ever visited, much less lived in, the Hamptons would know his family's name.

"It's right there on the Montauk Highway, the main road into the Hamptons, a big sign, you can't miss it, there's no way," Mr. Pompous insisted, clearly becoming more agitated by the second.

"No, sorry, I'm not familiar with it," maintained the Client CEO.

"You absolutely have to have seen it," Mr. Pompous continued, a dog not letting go of a bone. "It's right there, prominently displayed on the Montauk Highway, the main artery into the Hamptons, can't miss it. You have to drive by it. What route do you take to get into the Hamptons?"

The Client CEO's response: "I take a helicopter."

WHAM! Mic drop. Talk about getting grounded.

Mr. Pompous was one-upped and put in his place. He had no response, just a bit of muttering under his breath.

Chapter 11: Partyman

This story doesn't reflect the insurance industry's proudest moments, but it's somewhat amusing, so I'm including it. And while this book offers no lessons in insurance underwriting (Cue the shameless plug: I've written another book that does that), claims handling, marketing, or any other honorable aspect of the profession, it does provide some limited insights into the age-old art of grifting. So those of you who are interested in scamming people (and who isn't?), listen up!

At AIG in the mid-1990s, we had a colleague who was a little off the rails at times, as I believe he'd admit. I'm happy to say he eventually righted the ship and has gone on to be a prominent and very successful member of the industry. And he's a great guy, and a great father to his two sons; he's hitting home runs, figuratively anyway, on the regular these days. However, that wasn't always the case; for a while he was striking out in the game of life. And his future didn't look all that bright at the time.

Let's turn back the clock to the, in retrospect, amusing part of his life.

This individual, who I will refer to as Partyman (in another effort to avoid litigation), had a tendency to indulge, actually overindulge would be more accurate, in various mind-altering substances, including alcohol.

Back in those days, the mid-1990s, AIG would pay employees every other Thursday, usually with a direct deposit into their bank account. (Semi-related note: My friend Jason Hawkins of AXA XL and I used to have a running joke about people who were old-fashioned and slow to adapt to new ways. We'd say things like, "Where's William?" "Oh, he's depositing his paycheck." Or "He's waiting for a fax," or "He's using a payphone." You probably had to be there...).

Anyway, back to the story.

During one stretch, Partyman failed to show for work on the Friday after payday for six or eight consecutive pay periods. The pattern was fairly evident to even casual observers; he was blowing his paycheck every other Thursday night, partying hard, and then he was not able to drag himself out of bed for work the next morning. His finances were so tight because of his lavish spending on partying that if anyone wanted to contact him at home (this was before cell phones were common), they'd have to phone a Korean grocery store one floor below his Manhattan apartment, and a worker there would yell upstairs for him to come down to take the call. Yes, really.

On one post-payday Friday, Partyman did show up for work, but all banged up, as they say. He was pale, obviously in discomfort and complained of chest pains to one of his colleagues. She knew that he had been out very late the night before with some of our AIG colleagues, and she told him that he was simply hungover from a hard night of partying. But Partyman vigorously protested her allegations. He claimed to be having a heart attack. Eager to call his bluff, the colleague said, "Oh, OK, should I call an ambulance, then?" Partyman, in great distress and probably not thinking clearly, said, "Yeah, OK." So, she did.

About 20-minutes later, that colleague watched in astonishment as two EMTs carried Partyman past her cubicle on a stretcher. They apparently took him to the hospital to get relief from his massive hangover.

When Partyman showed up for work on Monday, he would not let go of his story. He claimed he had indeed suffered a heart attack but was now in good enough shape to return to work on Monday. The Miracles of Modern Medicine!

Another trick in his repertoire: Partyman regularly borrowed small amounts of money from AIG colleagues and then failed to repay them. Most of our colleagues, I believe, just immediately wrote off whatever money they loaned him, figuring they'd never see it again. However, to secure even larger amounts from victims, Partyman used a clever ruse. I'm not sure if it was his own invention, or if he had learned of it from another source, possibly Grifter U., but it worked well the first few times – until coworkers caught on and stopped participating.

Here's how it worked: Partyman would go from cubicle to cubicle at the AIG office in which he worked (I won't specify which one, just to add to the difficulty of any libel lawyers threatening to come after me...) and would tell people he was going to order a bunch of pizzas for lunch. Then he'd ask if they would like to chip in $10 to be a part of this group.

In the beginning, the majority of colleagues would participate, giving Partyman $10 each. Then, with a fat fistful of tens, Partyman would call a local pizzeria and order two or three pizzas, not nearly enough for the large number of people who had chipped in. He would pay for the two or three pizzas when delivered, and then he'd pocket the leftover money. Partyman's beer fund had been replenished!

When people showed up to the designated conference room to grab some pizza, they'd be unpleasantly surprised to find only a couple of empty boxes, Partyman would say, "Sorry, you got here too late, all the pizza is gone."

I'm not sure how he'd explain the fact that only two empty boxes remained, maybe he told victims that he had already thrown away the other empties. I, myself, never fell victim to this ruse, but had I worked in that office regularly, I probably would have been burned by this cheesy ruse (pun certainly intended). Regardless, whatever he said, it worked – for a while. Eventually, everyone realized what was going on and the Pizza Scam no longer worked in that office. Further proof that all good things must come to an end.

However, I'm happy to report that these days Partyman is so successful that he can buy his own pizza – and even an entire pizzeria if he'd like. All's well that ends well. And, of course, now that I've publicly revealed the Pizza Scam, perhaps one or more of you will keep it going. All in the interest of reenacting history, of course.

Chapter 12: Harrah's Golf –
Wandering in the Desert

Sometimes, fairly frequently actually, insurance people get to do fun things, like attending major sporting events, eating at trendy restaurants, playing golf, and going to nice resorts in warm-weather climates for conferences.

When I was at ACE in the early 2000s, we wrote the D&O Insurance on Harrah's, the large gaming and hospitality company based in Las Vegas. After one renewal, the risk manager at the time, Lance Ewing, invited me and my boss, Tim O'Donnell, out to Vegas to play a round of golf at Harrah's private course, named Cascata. "Cascata" means "waterfall" in Italian, in case you're an uncultured slob and, like me, didn't know that.

One of Cascata's claims to fame was that it was the only golf course in America (maybe the world) that boasted that when you were playing on any of its holes, you could not see any of the course's other holes. Each hole was nestled in its own little valley and provided a genuine feeling of isolation and exclusivity. Sick of seeing the hoi polloi yukking it up on an adjacent hold at your local muni? Not a concern at Cascata, thank you. And pass the Grey Poupon while you're at it.

There were a lot of unique and cool features at Cascata, including a stream (part of the waterfall Cascata is named after, one would presume) that ran under the clubhouse and was visible under a glass floor (we used to have glass ceilings in the insurance industry, but not anymore, now we have glass floors!)

When we arrived for the round of golf, we found our names engraved on metal plates affixed to our designated lockers in the men's locker room. When we completed the round, we were given metal nameplates as souvenirs. (It turns out they were affixed by magnets to the lockers; we were not being given permanent membership, unfortunately.) This was high-class living, my friends!

And unlike many low-roller country clubs, the player was king at Cascata and almost everything was allowed. There were no stodgy rangers patrolling the course to ensure you weren't taking too long, or that you didn't drive your golf cart too close to the greens. At Cascata, you were allowed to drive your golf cart RIGHT ONTO THE GREENS! Yes, really.

Cascata, I was told, was designed to lure "whales" (i.e., big gamblers) to Harrah's, and the company went to great lengths to make the experience memorable for these high-stakes gamblers, including sending private jets to the whales' local airports to bring them to Las Vegas. Must be nice. And, presumably, after they lost big sums, those same private jets would take them home. As a general rule, whales do not ride Greyhound Buses.

At the time, in the early 2000s, the rumor was that Cascata was inflicting somewhere in the neighborhood of a $3 million annual loss on Harrah's books, but that number probably paled in comparison to the tens of millions (if not more) gambled away by the whales who enjoyed playing there. Note: I think I lost $200 at the roulette wheel on that visit. I guess I'd be classified as a minnow, or possibly a guppy. But, nonetheless, we were gifted a round at Cascata by virtue of providing Harrah's Board of Directors with D&O Insurance.

At about the 14th hole of our round of golf, I sliced my drive far to the right. It landed on the sand among the cacti and various rocks and other desert plant life. Lance, the affable and sharp risk manager of Harrah's at the time, came up with one of the funniest lines I've ever heard on a golf course, which is probably why I still remember it 20-plus years later. Although, I'm betting that he did not create the line himself, and he'd probably used it many times before that day. Anyway, Lance yelled out to me from his spot on the fairway, "Hey Larry, are you Jewish?"

"No, I'm not," I yelled, "Why do you ask?" (I naively thought that maybe that day was a Jewish holiday or something.)

"Because you've spent all day wandering in the desert!"

Insert guffaws here.

I laughed at the time, it was a pretty good line but, unfortunately, I've never had occasion to use it on anyone else (I don't play a lot of desert golf). Perhaps you will be able to use it someday. Another fringe benefit of reading this book!

CHAPTER 13: THE TOP DOG LOUNGE

As people who know me can attest, especially my sister Maria, I'm a big fan of practical jokes. I don't know what my fair share of them would be, but I've no doubt played more than that amount over the years. And believe it or not, despite the insurance industry's stodgy public image, practical jokes are somewhat welcome – if they're not too extreme or played too often. Most bosses are usually happy to have their employees inject some humor into the workday – on an occasional basis.

This one is my personal favorite of the many practical jokes that I've perpetrated in an insurance work environment. [Note: My favorite all-time practical joke was when I worked at a soda distributor during summers in college. I made two forklift drivers briefly believe that they'd won $11 million in the New Jersey Lottery. They proceeded to gleefully inflict hundreds of dollars of damage on the warehouse by throwing 2-liter soda bottles everywhere, until a co-worker told them that I had pranked them. At which point, of course, they wanted to inflict physical harm on me. But that's a story for another book...]

This one occurred while I was an underwriting manager at ACE, which has since evolved into Chubb. I drafted a fictitious memo to our 40 or so underwriters on April Fool's Day in 2004. The memo purported to be from the ACE USA Travel Department, and it detailed a new travel initiative designed to reduce costs. Employees everywhere have received so many of these "We need to cut costs" directives that the memo appeared to be nothing out of the ordinary. At first, anyway.

I had my assistant, Helena Barber, distribute the memo via an e-mail to ACE's Professional Risk Group. And, I must say, Helena was quite a willing accomplice. Everyone in our group knew me and my propensity for humor well enough that they would've questioned the memo's authenticity if it came directly from me, so by sending it under Helena's email address, it aroused less suspicion. Here's what it said:

From: ACE USA Corporate Travel Department TL33P

Date: April 1, 2004

Re: New Travel Policy

CC: ACE USA Senior Executive Team

As most of you know, fuel costs have been rising rapidly and, along with them, the price of airline tickets. In order to avoid this unacceptable increase in travel costs, the ACE USA Travel Department has contracted with Greyhound Bus Lines to provide preferential terms to ACE USA. Effective immediately, all ACE USA business travel within 500 miles of one's office must be via Greyhound Bus Lines, unless the traveler produces an

"Authorization for Travel Exception" form signed by a company president and Vladimir Kramden of ACE Corporate Travel. Thus, for example, travelers in the Philadelphia headquarters would use Greyhound for all trips to Boston, New York, Washington, DC, Pittsburgh, and Cleveland.

Our negotiated agreement with Greyhound includes free access for all ACE USA travelers to the Greyhound Top Dog Lounges, which are located in the Greyhound terminals of most major cities. As a general rule of thumb, any city with an NHL franchise will have a Top Dog Lounge. These are member-only luxury lounges with free coffee, crumb cake (on weekdays only) and an assortment of complimentary newspapers, as well at least one conference table per lounge (some have more). We would encourage you to arrange your broker and client meetings at the Top Dog Lounge in destination cities, as it will facilitate a faster turn-around when facing a long bus trip home. You may also use the Top Dog Lounge when traveling on personal matters.

An initial ACE Focus Group using Greyhound had complained of some unsavory odors on some of the buses. Greyhound has assured us that the first three rows of every bus will be reserved for corporate travelers (you must show your ACE ID, which you will also use to gain access to the Top Dog Lounges). Greyhound's studies show that its customers who don't bathe regularly tend to ride near the back of the bus, so it shouldn't be an issue for us. Also, on bus trips of less than 200 miles, ACE travelers will be allowed to request an FM radio station of their choice. All in all, your shorter business trips should now be more economical, efficient, and enjoyable. Thanks for your cooperation in this most important ACE USA initiative.

Believe it or not, multiple people called Helena to complain that they had already booked a plane reservation for a business trip, and they refused to switch to Greyhound. A surprising number of employees, surprising to me anyway, were enraged at the new policy – until they realized that they'd been taken by an April Fool's joke. One person, upon learning the truth, tried to lecture Helena (unsuccessfully) about the impropriety of her participation in such a ruse. If you know Helena, you know where she told that person to go (Hint: It wasn't to a Top Dog Lounge and there was no free crumb cake involved.).

As an aside – I know, you're thinking, "This whole book has been an aside!" – I created the name "Vladimir Kramden" as a subtle tip of the hat to comedy's most iconic bus driver, Jackie Gleason as Ralph Kramden, in the sitcom classic "The Honeymooners." Very few people seized upon that clue, although I know you would have, dear reader, since you were insightful enough to purchase this book. Somewhere at the Big Bus Depot in The Sky, I hope ole Ralphie Boy got a chuckle out of that one. I know I did.

CHAPTER 14: HE EVEN RODE HIS MOTORCYCLE IN THE RAIN

The National Union Financial Institutions Group, at one point in the late 1990s, was growing robustly. We had hired about 10 underwriters in a fairly short period. Many of these new folks didn't know each other or any of their new AIG colleagues. I decided to facilitate the integration of the new hires with the old guard by running a game or contest that would help people get to know one another a bit better.

I hit upon the idea of conducting a contest where each of the 50 or so underwriters in our home office in downtown NYC would submit a little-known and unique fact about themselves to my assistant. She would then compile a contest entry form consisting of every underwriter's name on the left side of a page and the anonymous unique facts on the right side. The winner would be the person who correctly matched the most underwriters to their unique fact.

My assistant set up a pizza-and-soda lunch for the underwriters in a large conference room at which I would reveal each correct answer one-by-one and we'd hear a bit about the fact from the person who submitted it and then, at the end of the lunch, and we would crown our champion, that being the person with the most correct guesses.

I thought this game would be especially useful because after it was over, it would spur conversation among the group as people approached each other in the hallway and said things like, "I didn't know you were an extra in the movie 'Scent of a Woman,'" or "I didn't know that Greek was your first language as a kid.' (Both were actual facts from the contest; the second was mine.)

These unique facts seemed like they'd be a natural conversation starter among our colleagues, new and old alike. And, as an added bonus, most of the facts were actually fairly interesting.

But there were some exceptions.

Most notably, the "unique fact" proffered by then-underwriter (now broker) Mike Kambos. (Note: He's still in the industry and has given me permission to use his name. Maybe in the future, his interesting fact will be that his name is in this book!)

Mike had some convoluted and boring story about getting his truck stuck in the mud once. Really, that was it; there was no interesting aspect to it at all. The truck wasn't on fire, Kim Kardashian wasn't riding in the truck bed, and O.J. Simpson was not in Mike's truck's passenger seat avoiding the police.

<u>That was it, just a truck stuck in the mud</u>. You don't know how much of a favor I'm doing for you by not reprinting a transcript of the actual long-and-boring story.

I found it somewhat amusing, however, that Mike had such a mundane story/fact compared to most of the others. I was so taken by his story, in fact, that when I received Mike as my person in our group's Secret Santa game that Christmas, I gave him a small box, about the size of a watch box, which was filled with mud. I had embedded a Hot Wheels truck in this mud. It amused me and, apparently, Mike, too, since he kept it on his desk for years and recently told me that he still has it.

But the story doesn't end there. No, this story isn't quite as boring as the mere tale of a Kardashian-less truck stuck in mud.

Years after the Stuck in The Mud story, Mike and I, by then at different companies, were having a business lunch at a restaurant on Long Island. And before I go further, this might be hard to believe, but this story is <u>100 percent true</u>. If this story isn't true, then my name is Mud. Err, well, maybe that's not the best analogy here.

Anyway, during our lunch, Mike casually said, "My dad used to have a motorcycle repair shop just down the road here."

"Oh, really? Most Greeks of our parents' generation, the ones I know anyway, were in the diner business, like my father," I said.

"Yeah," Mike continued, "My father's business was pretty successful. I worked there sometimes. In fact, I repaired quite a few motorcycles, including a few for Billy Joel. In fact, I helped make a motorcycle for him."

The fork fell out of my mouth.

"Wait, what?" I said, "You repaired Billy Joel's motorcycles and the most interesting fact you could come up with for our game at AIG was that your truck once got stuck in the mud? Are you kidding me?!"

"Ah, I guess I just didn't think of it at the time," Mike said, as he shrugged and continued eating his lunch.

The lesson here: sometimes, the "dirtiest" story is not the best one to tell. As gossip columnist Cindy Adams says, "Only in New York, kids, only in New York."

Chapter 15: Not A Shred of Decency

As you've picked up by now, I like a good practical joke. More specifically, I like to be the one who <u>plays the practical joke</u> – although I don't mind being on the receiving end of a good one, either. Just not too often.

When I worked at Marsh in San Francisco in the mid-1990s, one of our senior brokers in the New York office, Kirk Jensen, came to visit our office. He had various meetings with clients in San Francisco. Kirk was a very knowledgeable guy (and still is) and clients generally enjoyed discussing coverage issues, market conditions and other industry topics with him.

I knew Kirk a bit, but we weren't best buddies or anything. However, unluckily for him, we were friendly enough that I felt comfortable pranking him.

On this particular day, Kirk had a late-afternoon client meeting somewhere in our office building, after which he was heading straight to the airport to catch his red-eye flight back to NYC. Shortly before his meeting, he came into my office and asked if I'd mind if he left his luggage and briefcase there while he was meeting with the clients. Of course, I said yes.

Shortly after Kirk left for his meeting, I had to go into our copy room to pick up some documents I had sent to the printer (I wasn't a Big Shot with my own printer). While in the copy room, I noticed a big, heavy stapler and my first thought was, "I'll hide this in Kirk's briefcase as a prank. He won't discover it until he gets to New York." But my wonderful boss at the time, Lisa Doherty (who has gone on to even greater insurance heights than being my boss!) was in the room, and she said it would be an annoyance if we didn't have that big stapler around to staple thick stacks of paper. Also, Kirk might have detected it in his briefcase since it was so heavy.

She was right on both counts.

Airport security in those pre-9/11 days wasn't as strict as today, but the stapler might have been detected in Kirk's luggage before he boarded.

After this idea was shot down, I noticed the big garbage can stuffed full of shredded paper in the room. Inspiration struck! I grabbed two big handfuls of the shredded paper and went back to my office and jammed them into Kirk's briefcase. The shredded paper wasn't heavy, and it would not be noticeable until Kirk opened the briefcase. On paper (pun partially intended), this seemed like a great gag.

Soon thereafter, Kirk came by my office and picked up his briefcase and luggage and raced off to SFO.

The next morning, I came into the office and played a voicemail message Kirk had left me.

"Larry, I know it was you. I was on the plane, and it was about 2 a.m. and I couldn't sleep, so I decided to do some work. I opened my briefcase and, as you can imagine, I was shocked to find a bunch of shredded paper tumbling out. My first thought was, 'Oh, no, Goanos shredded all the papers in my briefcase!' When I realized that you only <u>added</u> shredded paper and had not actually shredded my documents that were in the briefcase, I was very happy and quite relieved. Good one!'"

That's me, a real cut-up.

Chapter 16: A Light Bulb Goes Off

This story involves an insurance law firm, not a carrier or broker, but law firms comprise an important part of the insurance industry and I'm happy to include them in this book.

There are a number of top-notch insurance defense law firms in the industry, including, but certainly not limited to: Aguilar Bentley; Anderson Kill; Bailey Cavalieri; Blank Rome; Clyde & Co; Cohen Ziffer Frenchman & McKenna; Cole Scott & Kissane; Cooper Levenson; Coughlin Betke; Covington & Burling; Cozen O'Connor; Day Pitney; GoldbergSegalla (yes, no space between names, I checked!); Gordon, Rees, Scully Mansukhani; Hamilton, Miller & Birthisel; Hinshaw & Culbertson; Haynes and Boone; Kaufman Borgeest & Ryan; Kaufman Dolowich; Kennedys; Lewis Brisbois Bisgaard & Smith; London Fischer; Manire Galla Curley; Margolis Edelstein; Marshall Dennehey Warner Coleman & Goggin; McCarter & English; Mendes and Mount; Mintzer Sarowitz Zeris & Willis; Morrison Mahoney; Mound Cotton Wollen & Greengrass; O'Hagan Meyer; Peabody & Arnold; Perkins Coie; Proskauer; Rebar Kelly; Reed Smith; Squire Patton Boggs; Thompson Coe; Traub Lieberman Straus & Shrewsberry; Rivkin, Radler; Tucker, Dyer & O'Connell; Tyson & Mendes; Vanek, Larson & Kolb; Wiley Rein; Wilson, Elser; and Winget, Spadafora & Schwartzberg. Phew!

Back in the early 1990s, when I was practicing law (I practiced a lot, but never perfected it), I took a job with the Boston law firm of Parker, Coulter, Daley & White. PCD&W is no longer with us – it disbanded in the mid-1990s – but it employed a lot of excellent lawyers and paralegals, including (again, alphabetically) Chris Betke, Rick Connolly, Bill Cotter (R.I.P.), Jason Cotton, Emily Coughlin, Maynard Kirpilani, Kristin Kraeger, Gina Leahy, Brian O'Connell; Joe O'Neil (not that one, the other), Scott Richardson, John Rodman, Mark Rosen (ditto, the other one), Jack Ryan (again, not the famous one you're thinking of), Joe Schmick, Scott Tucker and Jay Sicklick.

I started at the firm in early 1990. My law school friend Chris Betke had been working there for a few years by the time I joined. On my first day, I was shown to my new office, where affixed to the front of the desk was the word "W-E-L-C-O-M-E," spelled out on Post-It Notes ™, one letter per sheet. (Note: By using that ™ symbol, it looks like I'm actually paying attention to copyright laws, etc., which I am not, but perception can be reality, as we all know.)

Chris came into my new office on my first day to welcome me to the firm in person. All seemed well.

About a day or two later, I came back from lunch to find a handwritten note on a legal pad sitting on my desk chair. It said, "Larry, come see me," and was purportedly signed by Paul Kelly, the managing partner of our 100-lawyer firm. Paul's specialty was worker's compensation law – he had nothing to do with professional lines, my specialty – so I was immediately suspicious of the note. I didn't know Chris's handwriting well enough to determine if he had written it, so I marched into his office and showed it to him.

"Did you write this?" I asked in an accusatorial tone.

"No, not me," he said. I grilled him six ways to Sunday, and he kept denying that he'd written it. Finally, I figured that I'd better not risk ignoring the firm's managing partner during my first week of employment, so I walked down to Paul's large corner office. His assistant, who sat outside his office, said he was on the phone but that I could go in to see him.

I had brought the legal pad with me to show the note to Paul since I was suspicious that it might be a prank. I walked into Paul's office and saw him speaking on the phone. He looked up at me and I quietly mouthed, "Paul, did you want to see me?" and I showed him the note on the legal pad.

He softly laughed and mouthed the word, "No," before shooing me away with his hand. As I suspected, I had been duped.

I immediately marched back to Chris' office (when people are angry, I feel like they "march" more than just walk) and confronted him.

"Paul said he didn't write the note!"

Chris laughed and said, "I got you. I wrote the note!"

Mutha......!!!!!

I said, "Chris, I specifically confronted you about this, I suspected that you had written it, and you denied it. You lied to me."

"Yeah, well, I got you," he said.

Game on, like Donkey Kong.

Our offices were in a building in downtown Boston at One Beacon Street (Interesting Trivia: The One Beacon Street address would later become the inspiration for the name of the insurance company One Beacon, which, I believe, was headquartered in the building).

The management company for the One Beacon Street building, R.M. Bradley, had offices few floors above us. A couple of days after I had started, the woman who ran our law firm's administrative operations told me that I'd have to go upstairs to get my photo taken and my building I.D. card made in R.M. Bradley's offices.

I went upstairs and a nice lady took my photo and created my I.D. card. Shortly after returning to my office, Chris came in. I had received a desk lamp a few days earlier, along with the rest of the initial office supplies that I had ordered on my first day at the firm. Upon seeing my desk lamp, Chris had decided that he too needed more light at his desk, so he had ordered one also. My desk lamp had come with a florescent light bulb in it, but for some inexplicable reason, when Chris got his desk lamp, there was no light bulb in the box.

"Hey, where did you get the bulb for your desk lamp?" he asked. "Mine came today but there was no bulb."

Thinking quickly and drawing upon the fact that I had just returned from R.M. Bradley's offices upstairs, I said, "R.M. Bradley, they have all the desk lamp bulbs up there."

"What? Why would they have them?" he asked, a bit suspicious of my answer.

"I don't know," I said, "I guess because they manage the building and buy the overhead lights for all the fixtures. They probably get discounts on all the lighting, including the desk lamps," I said.

The inspiration for this clever lie had just struck me out of the blue, I have no explanation for it. It was very similar, I would imagine, to the process that led Einstein to came up with the Theory of Relativity. On a more localized scale, of course. And of a much immature and inane nature. And it provided absolutely no benefit to society. But, otherwise, the thought processes were exactly the same!

About five minutes after leaving my office, Chris came marching (there's that word again) back into my office. "You mother-effer!"

he said, "They didn't have desk lamp bulbs up there! I told the receptionist that I was from Parker, Coulter and that I needed a bulb for my desk lamp...and she just looked at me in bewilderment, like I had two heads. Then I realized that you had gotten me. You suck!"

Well, in my book – and this is my book – we were even!

CHAPTER 17: SARA-TOGA...TOGA...TOGA NATIONAL!

People in the insurance industry can occasionally (OK, maybe frequently) let down their hair and have fun in unorthodox ways. This story chronicles one of those times. For you, dear reader, no toga is required to read this story... but it might help.

As you've gleaned by now, if you didn't already know it, the insurance industry is rife with entertaining events of all kinds, including, and some might say especially, golf outings. When I was at ACE in the early 2000s, we established a bit of a tradition of taking a group of insurance brokers to the horse races at Saratoga Race Course (yes, that's the official name; I Googled it) in Upstate New York in August for a day at the races. Between our insurance broker guests and our ACE employees, we'd have about 30 people at the event. We'd arrive a day early and play a round of golf at Saratoga National Golf Club, an awesome facility not far from the horse track.

One year, we had finished our round of golf and, after freshening up, everyone gathered on the second floor of the Saratoga National clubhouse for a cocktail hour before dinner. There was a large balcony off the cocktail hour room that could accommodate all 30 of us. It overlooked the outdoor dining patio on the ground floor. About 20 yards beyond the patio was the course's 18th hole.

I don't know why this cockamamie idea came to me (alcohol could have been a catalyst and/or that genius Albert Einstein-way-of-thinking from the previous story), but during the cocktail hour, I decided it would be a good idea to hold an impromptu "Closest To The Pin Contest" using the 18th hole as our target.

But this contest was not a "Closest to the Pin" competition in the traditional sense. That would involve hitting golf balls, which would have been impractical; let's not be ridiculous here, folks! Rather, the contest involved <u>throwing</u> the balls from the large balcony – and over the heads of people dining on the patio – to the nearby 18th green. Well, hopefully the throws would go over the diners' heads, since a misfire could have ended up in someone's gazpacho.

Believe it or not, ACE senior management at the event (whose names I'll withhold to protect their careers which have been otherwise filled with great decision making) agreed to go along with this bats***-crazy idea. But I guess that's obvious, otherwise this story wouldn't be in the book. "I had a crazy idea and senior management squashed it," doesn't generate a lot of interest among readers. I have to give kudos to the ACE senior managers at the event for being so flexible, forward-thinking and fun.

My idea was to have each participant – and all 30 attendees played along – chip in $10 toward the pot. Then, after they paid their money, each person would get a golf ball, upon which they would write their initials with a Sharpie. We'd all throw the balls one at a time from the balcony to the 18th green (again, hopefully clearing the heads of the people eating below) and the person whose ball ended up closest to the pin would take the entire pot, $300 in cash (note to any IRS agents reading this: Proper tax forms were filed).

As we started throwing the balls, one at a time, the diners realized something was going on above them. They began looking up. I think most reasonable people, while dining on the outside patio of a tony golf club, would not expect to see a group of supposedly respectable and well-dressed businesspeople (emphasis on "supposedly") throwing golf balls over their heads. So, as you might imagine, there was a bit of a stir among the high-end clientele. You can dress insurance people up, but ...

The good news: None of the golf balls hit any patrons of the club's restaurant, nor did any balls land on the patio. Everyone's throw reached the green, thankfully. It was a bit slippery on the balcony and one guy, whose name I won't mention (cough, cough, Wes Wolfe) slipped and fell on his back as he threw. But fortunately, he wasn't injured (I don't know if we carried Workers' Comp for the event). And, even more fortunately, his ball cleared the patio.

I believe the last ball had just been thrown when one of the club's employee/bouncers (well, I don't think high-end golf clubs actually employ bouncers, but Saratoga National might have started doing so after that night) ascended the stairs to the second floor and told us to knock it off. Too late, we were done. Then, one of the junior underwriters ran downstairs to gather all 30 golf balls and to tell us who had won the contest with the closest to the pin toss.

Now, before I tell you who won, allow me to say a few words about my former boss at ACE, Dave Lupica.

Dave is a great guy, truly, and was a terrific boss. His one annoying characteristic, to me anyway, was his uncanny ability to <u>always</u> win at golf. Granted, he is a pretty talented golfer, and he used to have a handicap in the single digits (it might still be, I don't know; for some strange reason he doesn't golf with me these days...), but his prowess at winning at golf competitions is unsurpassed. I'd say it's his Superpower. If aliens ever land on Earth from Planet AugustaZor and demand to challenge our best golfer to a match, I ain't nominating Tiger Woods, or Rory McIlroy, any of those PGA or LIV stiffs. I'm pushing for Dave Lupica to be our man. He'd prevail, I'm sure. The mofo just can't lose.

Once, and this is 100 percent true (everything else in the book is true too; I feel impelled to specifically say that a story in this book is true, however, whenever it sounds like BS on its face), I witnessed Dave's foursome fail to finish among the top three at an insurance golf outing. Once. It was run by Aon's Philadelphia office in 2003 or so. Now, full disclosure, Dave's foursome probably didn't finish in the money because I was in it. HOWEVER, and again, this is absolutely true, following the round of golf and the subsequent dinner, there was a raffle of various door prizes. Dave, I shat you not, won a big-screen TV in the raffle. It almost didn't fit in his car.

Even on the rare occasion that Dave doesn't earn his way onto a stage to accept a golfing prize because of his golfing prowess, he still finds a way to win something.

I am convinced the man is incapable of losing in any golf-related competition. And, yes, it does piss me off, obviously, since I'm writing about it in this book!

Now, back to the original story. As you have figured out by now, when the young underwriter bounded up the stairs to the second-floor dining room where we were all awaiting the winner's name, he held up the winning ball above his head and loudly announced, "Dave Lupica!"

Boo!

The rich get richer folks, ain't it always the way.

But it was an extremely enjoyable outing – we had a blast – and just another of the fun adventures you get with an insurance career kids!

CHAPTER 18: FORK IT OVER

By now you've REALLY gathered that I like practical jokes. I enjoy
playing them. You might, too. This one occurred many years ago
at AIG's annual Stowe Cup, a yearly skiing event sponsored by AIG
at Stowe Mountain in Vermont, which AIG owned at the time; I'm
not sure if they still do. This is a practical joke you don't see a lot –
I may have created it, I'm honestly not sure – but it's a good one,
and it's yet another example of something in this book that by
itself is worth your purchase price. And I say that with complete
impartiality, of course.

In the 1990s (and possibly still today), certain senior managers at
AIG were invited to the AIG Ski Cup every year. We were told to
invite along some of the brokers who brought us the most business,
and policyholder's who paid the biggest premiums.

My colleagues in the Financial Institutions Group of National
Union (I'll spare you the entire lengthy name of National Union.)
(Of course, now I realize it would've been shorter to write it out
than to explain that I'm sparing you the full name) and I invited
the insurance risk management team of Fidelity Investments.
Fidelity was a big client of AIG's at the time, purchasing a wide
variety of our products and paying millions of dollars in premiums
annually.

The head insurance risk manager of Fidelity was a legendary figure named Judy Lindenmayer (R.I.P.). Judy was one of the true characters in the history of the insurance industry. An entire book could be written about Judy. She was possibly the first woman to ever receive the ARM designation, which stands for Associate in Risk Management. She was also renowned for rolling the bones at nearby casinos whenever possible on business trips. In addition, she did things like throwing such a raucous party at her suburban Boston house once that her Marsh brokers had to re-hang a couple of shutters that had fallen off the house during the party (it's true!)

Alas, Judy did not come on this particular ski trip – I don't think she was a skier – but a few of her lieutenants did, including Tom Wronski, Peter Burd and Kelly Ravanis (three more books sold!)

One night during the Ski Cup, a large group of AIG and Fidelity people went to dinner at a Mexican restaurant in Stowe. I don't remember the name of it, but I think it had one of those seemingly-clever-but-now-overused names with a cultural juxtaposition, something like Paco Murphy's or Pedro O'Hara's or Juan Finnegan's (I could go on with examples, but I'll spare you, much like I didn't type out National Union Fire Insurance Company of Pittsburgh, PA above.) OK, interlude here: Curiosity got the best of me, and I just Googled the Mexican restaurant in Stowe; it appears to no longer be around. Se la vie Alejandro Stein's...

Anyway, about 15 or so of us were finishing dinner at Declan Fernandez's when Kelly got up to go to the ladies' room. The restaurant was empty except for our party. I was sitting directly across from Kelly and, out of nowhere, a devilish inspiration hit me. Actually, I say "out of nowhere," but I seem to have a large reservoir of devilish inspiration within me, so it must come from somewhere (see, e.g., the story at the end of this book).

Kelly had made the fatal mistake – among this group anyway – of leaving her pocketbook on her chair when she departed for the ladies' room. I immediately asked everyone at the table to pass me any clean silverware that was near them. Note: I do have a heart people, and I made sure to only use <u>clean</u> silverware for this stunt. I gathered the eight or 10 pieces of cutlery and unzipped Kelly's pocketbook and jammed them inside before zipping it back up.

Next, to complete the set up for this prank, which I hope you will consider trying in the future on a valued client or vendor, or maybe at your grandmother's 95th birthday party, I called the waiter over to our table and said, "We're playing a joke on the young lady who owns this pocketbook. When we start to leave the restaurant after we pay, please stop us and say that you believe some silverware has been stolen and that you would like to check her pocketbook. We put a bunch of cutlery in there as a joke. We will leave an extra-large tip if you go along with this."

I find that whenever playing a practical joke involving waitstaff, the inclusion of "an extra-large tip" usually induces compliance, as it did in this instance.

Kelly returned to the table, and everyone finished their drinks within a few minutes. An observation that will surprise none of you: At insurance dinners, drink glasses rarely remain anything other than empty at the end. Then, someone paid the bill with their AIG company credit card (Diner's Club, believe it or not), and we all got up to leave.

Just as we got to the restaurant's front door, when I thought that perhaps the waiter had forgotten about the prank and our bribe, he came racing out of nowhere to stop us. "I'm sorry," he said, "But it appears that some silverware is missing from your table. I would like to check this woman's pocketbook; we think it might be in there."

Kelly was taken aback at this brazen accusation.

I still remember her exact words, spoken loudly and earnestly: "I think not!"

With that, Kelly laid her pocketbook on its side on a nearby table and unzipped it. A bunch of silverware immediately came spilling out onto the table. We all roared with laughter, as her face turned bright red for a brief moment, before she realized that we had pranked her. And in short order she figured out that the main culprit behind this maneuver was me.

It was childish, yes, but it provided a few moments of mirth at the end of a long dinner, and it may even have strengthened our relationship with the people at Fidelity (except for Kelly, of course!). In addition, it is a story I still tell every once in a while. It is sort of a comedy annuity; it keeps paying dividends!

CHAPTER 19: SOME LIKE IT HOT

This is another of my favorite April Fool's Day jokes. It was perpetrated in the form of an email I wrote in 2007, only about two weeks after I had started a new job at Professional Indemnity Agency (PIA) in Mount Kisco, New York [the company is now a part of the huge Japanese insurer Tokio Marine.]

Recounting this email calls to mind advice my mother gave me long ago (My good friend, Tim Harrington, delights in recounting this at every opportunity since he witnessed it live.). A few days before I started my first job after law school, which was my first white-collar job ever, my mother admonished me: "Now Sonny, don't let your personality show for a few months." She feared, I believe, that I would be fired fairly quickly if I did not heed her advice. Unfortunately, I have never been able to fully comply with her words of wisdom.

Suspecting that my reputation as a prankster preceded me at PIA, I asked our Human Resources Director to send this e-mail to the roughly 75 employees in our offices. I knew that coming from her, the email would appear legit:

To: All New York PIA Employees

From: Human Resources

Date: April 1, 2007

Re: HVAC System Repairs

The Westchester County Department of Buildings (WCDB) has informed us that our HVAC (heating, ventilation and air conditioning) system is not up to code. WCDB says it will condemn 37 Radio Circle Drive if that is not corrected by November 1, 2007. The main problem is that our heating system is antiquated and needs a major overhaul. The connuter valve is totally shot and the Finnegan's Manifold hisses and sputters, as some of you who sit near it know. It doesn't have long either. The oscillating beta drive also needs replacement. If you've had this done at your home, you know how difficult this repair can be.

As a result of these upgrades, we will have technicians on site from next Wednesday until approximately 2 p.m. on October 15, 2007. While we expect minimal noise, General Electric says that the installation and testing of the heating equipment will require the building to be maintained at temperatures between 90 and 95 degrees on most days in order to achieve "laboratory conditions." Windows and doors will not be allowed to remain open as this compromises the required laboratory conditions. Management fully understands that this may be a bit uncomfortable, especially at the height of summer, but we have some helpful suggestions.

- Wear light clothing and open-toed shoes with no socks (men may wear tank tops but only those without NBA logos).
- Eat something cold for breakfast, like ice cream or a milk shake.
- Surround yourself with cooling pictures in your workspace (such as Arctic scenes or photos of skiers, icicles, etc.).
- York Peppermint Patties reportedly provide a "cooling sensation" so we will have bowls of those around the offices.

In addition to the above, we recommend that you remove from your workspace all candles, wax figures and any other items that may melt in extreme heat. We will also have a TV in the main conference room playing a DVD of the 1980 Winter Olympics in order to provide a place to get a cool break. The "Miracle on Ice" comes to PIA! Again, we apologize for any inconvenience these necessary repairs may cause, and we invite everyone to enjoy their April Fool's Day on Sunday!

I wrote that e-mail not knowing that the previous winter PIA had actually experienced problems with the HVAC system. Shortly after Stacey had hit "send," I stopped into the office of a longtime PIA employee named Buck (last name withheld to avoid litigation) who had weathered the previous year's HVAC problems. As I walked in, Buck was glaring at his computer screen, his face red and his blood pressure visibly rising.

"Larry, did you see this? I can't work in these conditions, this is insane. It's crazy!" Not wanting his blood on my hands if he passed out, I told Buck that it was an April Fool's joke before I became responsible for a death-by-heart-attack. Note: I've narrowly avoided causing a fatal seizure or stroke a few times with my pranks, so I have a prepared alibi always at the ready (which I've not had to use yet, knock wood, and I ain't revealing it here!)

CHAPTER 20: A CHEAP SHOT

This story occurred in the late 1990s at AIG. Among the group of underwriters that I managed were two gentlemen who had a couple of traits in common.

First, they were both from wealthy families.

Second, they were both cheap as s***.

They'd give you the sleeves out of their vests, as the old saying goes. When they opened their wallets, moths flew out and all the dead presidents squinted from finally seeing the light of day.

You get the idea.

I'll call them Brad and Jason (real first names) but I'll shield their identities a bit by not revealing their last names (although they're both probably still too cheap to hire lawyers to sue me...)

One day, I was reviewing the underwriting of an account with Jason when Brad sauntered into my office. He announced that he'd wait for me to finish with Jason as he took a seat on one of my visitor's chairs.

Jason and I had a momentary pause in our review of the account, so I asked, "How are things going with the flight attendant that you recently started dating?"

"Pretty good," he said, "In fact she came over to my apartment last night."

"Oh yeah, how did that go?" I asked.

"Not bad," Jason said. "I wanted her to come over, but not too early since then I might have to buy her dinner. So, I waited until about 9 o'clock, and then I paged her." (Note for you youngsters: This was in pre-cell phone days when you could dial a phone number to "page" someone and they'd see your phone number on the screen of their pager, so they'd know to call you. A pager was about half the size of a pack of cigarettes.)

"What happened then?" I asked.

"Well, I didn't want her to arrive and then ask right away to go out to a bar in the neighborhood, which could get pretty expensive. I had a bottle of wine in my fridge, so I had to figure out a way to keep her in my apartment and away from the expensive bars. Most people don't want to put their shoes back on again after taking them off, especially after a long day of work, so when she came in, I told her I just had my carpet steam-cleaned and asked her to take off her shoes, which she did."

"So how was the night?" I asked.

"Well," Jason said, "I'll just say that she didn't leave my place until 6 o'clock this morning."

"Hmm, pretty good," I responded, "But let me ask you a question: Was the carpet so clean that it was a plausible story to say it was recently steam cleaned?"

"No, actually, that was really the only flaw in my plan, the carpet didn't look very clean," Jason admitted.

"I know, I know," chimed in Brad, who had been sitting by quietly and just listening until then. "You should have dimmed the lights, that way she wouldn't have been able to see that the carpet didn't look recently steam cleaned. PLUS, you would have saved money on electricity!"

If Albert Einstein could have fathered two Geniuses of Cheapness, these would have been them. And I'm sure they'll see this story in this book after they each borrow a copy from someone; they certainly wouldn't shell out their own money for one!

CHAPTER 21: TELLING AN ENTIRE COMPANY TO "GO EFF YOURSELF"

In the late '90s, when I was in the Financial Institutions Group at AIG's National Union subsidiary, I was based in the New York City home office. One day, I had a morning underwriting meeting in Philadelphia. I took along a young underwriter and we drove from NYC in a rental car. On that day, our subsidiary president, John Keogh, was holding a company-wide conference call to discuss some important and highly complex insurance issue, which I won't tell you about here (since I can't remember what it was).

This was waaaaaaaay before the days when video conference calls were available. Yes, kids, some of us are still alive from those olde days! Trying to be a team player, I phoned into the conference call from my cell phone while in the rental car. There were about 500 people listening to the call from across the country. An administrative assistant who was handling the technical aspects of the call reminded everyone to put their phones on mute so that there would be no background noise distractions. I obediently did so.

Then, Murphy's Law kicked in. That Murphy is a mofo.

A few seconds after muting my phone, I received a call from our reinsurance broker in London. She was trying to place a difficult layer of reinsurance for us on a big account, and I needed to hear her update because the deal was scheduled to close soon.

Thus, I took my phone off mute and switched over to the other line to speak with her. Conveniently, I was stopped at a red light heading into the Holland Tunnel from the New Jersey side, so it made taking the call easier. When we finished talking, I switched my phone over to the nationwide conference-call line. However – and this is where Mr. Murphy suddenly appeared – before I could put the phone back on mute, and just as I rejoined the call, the traffic light turned green. As is the practice of many (a-hole) drivers in the New York Metropolitan Area, the guy behind me laid on his horn a split-second after the green light appeared. Literally, a split-second. Annoyed, I responded with a prolonged beep back at him and, as the horn blared, I turned to the underwriter in the passenger's seat and said, "You know what that means? That means 'Go eff yourself!'"

The administrative assistant running the nationwide conference call quickly announced, "Whoever just said 'Go eff yourself,' please put your phone on mute."

Oops!

Side Note: Honestly, I was a bit surprised that the admin guy actually said the phrase, "Go eff yourself," I would have expected him to just say something like, "Whoever just used profanity, please mute your phone." Perhaps, subconsciously, he too wanted to say, "Go eff yourself" to the entire company, but heretofore he never had a golden opportunity like this one. I served it up on a silver platter. And, who knows, maybe I saved him from years of therapy!

There were about 30 of my Financial Institutions Group colleagues in a conference room at our home office at the time of my slip of the tongue. One of them said, I later learned, "That sounded like Larry Goanos." Thankfully, my friend and then-AIG colleague Kirk Raslowsky, who probably never thought he'd get a shoutout for his good deed in a book 25 years later, immediately said, "No, no, that's not Larry, he's in Philly at a meeting, it can't be him." Thank you, Kirk!

About a year later, I told our company president, John Keogh, that it was me who had told almost our entire company to go eff themselves. To his credit, he shrugged it off and laughed. Thank you, John!

CHAPTER 22: A SUIT-ABLE COMMENT

You probably don't know Charles D'Andrea, a now-retired former Aon broker in the New York office. Take it from me, he's a great guy. He grew up in Pittsburgh and was a scholarship football player at Rutgers, long before Rutgers football was cool (throwing a bone to you RU fans out there, savor it!).

Perhaps because he is a great guy, and fairly unflappable, I have always enjoyed busting Charlie's chops whenever possible. There are three main types of guys (and, yes, it's almost always guys) whose chops I enjoy busting: 1. Good guys; 2. Jerks; and 3. Everyone in between. Charlie was usually in a serious mood – or he was back in his working days, anyway, I don't know how he is in his retirement, hopefully he's lightened up a bit. And he was always dignified and reserved. In short, he never acted like a boorish loudmouth, unlike a certain author of this book.

In the early 2000s, Fleet Bank was based in Boston. It was created by the 1999 merger of Fleet Financial Group and BankBoston. Fleet would go on to be acquired by, or "merged with" (as larger institutions like to say when buying a smaller one) Bank of America in 2004. I think this "merged with" verbiage is often used because the bigger company doesn't want to hurt any feelings at the target company. "Hey, we're equals, and we're just 'merging,' nobody is 'acquiring' you!" the bigger institution will say. This, of course, is bulls***. And it rings particularly hollow once the layoffs begin and most of the newly unemployed workers on the street looking for jobs were formerly with the smaller target company. These employees have now been "merged with" the unemployment line.

Calling such an acquisition a "merger" is especially important because offending the target company's executives by implying that they're a lesser company that is being taken over may result in hurting their feelings and them then needing a higher purchase price to make the deal work. I know, I know, you didn't expect interesting banking and psychological insights in this book. Although, I'm sure some would say you still didn't get any.

Back to the story.

Charlie was a professional lines insurance broker working on the Fleet account in the early 2000s. In 2004, he convened a meeting of all the underwriters on the account, about 15 people, at Fleet's Boston headquarters so the CFO could update all of its professional lines insurance carriers on the bank's performance. I was working at ACE (now Chubb, after a "merger" in 2016) at the time, and attended the meeting with one of our younger underwriters.

Charles had arranged for lunch for the underwriters to be brought into a large conference room at the bank's headquarters. Lunch was scheduled to precede the underwriting meeting. Now, in case you have some misconceptions about the quality of insurance conference-room lunches, please understand that I'm talking along the lines of soggy tuna and dried-out chicken sandwiches. Nothing fancy kids, sorry. Note: We do have nice meals at restaurants, but conference rooms never.

My colleague and I were running a bit late, and when we got to the floor where the meeting was, we immediately encountered Charlie and the bank's risk manager in a small room just off to the side of the conference room where the meeting would take place. As soon as I saw Charlie, purely in a generalized effort to bust his stones with no specific (or malicious) intent, I said, "There you are, Charlie, in your Armani suit, you're always the best-dressed guy in the insurance industry!"

Truth be known, I couldn't distinguish an Armani suit from a Bart Simpson brand suit if my life depended on it, but the comment just came to me at that moment, as I tried to bust Charlie. And it also seemed like a bit of a compliment because I was saying he was well dressed.

"Are you wearing your expensive Rolex, too?" I asked in a manner that was, admittedly, in a bit of a mocking tone. Charlie looked at me with obvious annoyance, bordering on disdain, and simply pointed us to the conference room where lunch was being served without saying anything.

A few days later, Charlie called me to explain what had happened. "Larry, your timing was horrific. When you came in and started ragging on me about wearing an Armani suit and having a Rolex, I was in the middle of negotiating my fee for the Fleet account with the risk manager. I'm pleading for more money and you're telling him I wear Armani suits!"

While he was somewhat annoyed with me, Charlie also found it rather amusing. I never learned if he managed to get his fee increased that year, but at least I got a story out of it for this book!

CHAPTER 23: LONG LIVE FREE SPEECH!

This book wasn't originally supposed to contain only stories from my career. Before I started writing it, I solicited funny and/or interesting insurance stories from my 4,000+ LinkedIn contacts, most of whom are in the insurance industry. In reply, I received exactly... one. Coincidentally, that one was from my friend Steve Pincus, Ryan's dad and a now-retired Willis executive. Believe it or not, Steve sent this story to me months before Ryan's tragic death, and, obviously, long before I decided to dedicate this book to Ryan's memory.

Steve told me the story of an insurance industry charity dinner to benefit all the wonderful work done by the United Jewish Appeal (UJA). Maurice R. "Hank" Greenberg, the legendary CEO of AIG and, later, Starr Companies, was tasked with landing a headline speaker for the dinner. Having no shortage of impressive contacts, Hank decided to call the legendary owner of the New York Yankees, George Steinbrenner, to solicit his participation.

According to the way Steve heard the story, Hank got George (I'm obviously on a first-name basis with people in this social stratum ... in my mind, anyway) on the phone and said, "George, how do you feel about free speech?"

George Steinbrenner reportedly replied, "Free speech? I'm all for it."

"Good," said Hank, "Because you're going to be giving one at the UJA charity dinner next month."

CHAPTER 24: SIX SIGMA STIGMA AT AIG

This story might give you a feel for the AIG of the 1990s and early 2000s, which was, in my Constitutionally protected free-speech opinion, a hard-charging, no-nonsense (well, a little nonsense), budget-focused grindery (I'm not sure if that's a word, but it should be.). I believe that the AIG of today is a far cry from that, much more genteel, civil and employee-friendly, but back in its 20th-Century heyday, AIG was a rampaging juggernaut, in many different ways.

In the late 1990s, there was a popular management method sweeping the United States known as Six Sigma. It was created in the 1980s by a guy named Bill Smith (not to be confused with the insurance industry's Bill Smith, RIP, formerly of AIG and Kemper) at Motorola. And, yes, I enlisted the aid of Mr. Google to get all that info as well.

Mr. Smith wasn't the CEO of Motorola at the time, but the guy who was, Bob Galvin, apparently supported the concept wholeheartedly. It was designed to be a tool to increase the quality and efficiency of business management, and it was quite a successful one at that. In 1988, Motorola won the Malcolm Baldridge National Quality Award, an honor given to organizations that demonstrate operational excellence. OK, OK, snoozefest over. For now.

In the 1990s, Six Sigma was popularized by General Electric and its legendary CEO, Jack Welsh. Six Sigma is still around (thanks again, Mr. Google), but it doesn't appear to be as popular as it once was. Perhaps this story will spark a raging comeback. You're welcome, Six Sigma.

I don't recall all the specifics of the Six Sigma program (sorry, I'm not Googling it again; do it yourself, if you're so interested, I'm busy writing a book here!), but the general thrust was to make companies and their employees more efficient. One of the big accounting/consulting firms, possibly Arthur Anderson, R.I.P. (it's in the same graveyard as Enron, Lehman Brothers, Reliance, et al.), assembled a team of consultants who went around the country training people on Six Sigma methods. Back in the late '90s, AIG hired this marauding band of corporate trainers (your next Uber driver may have been one of them) to provide Six Sigma lessons to a group of senior managers at its National Union (again, abbreviated name) subsidiary. I was among the lucky group chosen to participate. There were about 20 of us.

There was one, and only one, of the Six Sigma exercises that I remember vividly. After a seemingly endless cascade of tedious classroom lectures, mind-numbing PowerPoint presentations and other blah, blah, blahbery (and you think this book is boring!), our group was assembled in a conference room and seated at various stand-alone desks. They were the type you'd see in a high school, smallish and moveable. There were also a few long tables. All intentionally positioned for the Six Sigma-illuminating exercise.

We were told to imagine ourselves as managers overseeing a corporate mailroom. The trainers had various envelopes for us to use as props, and we were tasked with designing the most efficient methods to get the mail moving through various stations in the mailroom (e.g., sorting, weighing, stamping, etc.). The trainers timed our sessions, during which we physically moved this fictional mail through the process. The goal was to conceive innovations to reduce the amount of time it took to move the mail through the system. Note: Going postal on someone was not one of the options. Well, it wasn't supposed to be, anyway.

The person who was selected to play one of the messengers to ferry the mail between stations – which entailed walking briskly for about five or ten paces between desks – was not getting the job done quickly enough for our highly-critical AIG tastes. We later learned that, ideally, we should have solved this problem of slow mail delivery between stations by simply pushing the tables together so that the messenger wouldn't have to waste time walking from one table to another back-and-forth across the room. Had we pushed the tables together, there would be no need for a messenger to carry the mail at all; a person at one station would simply hand the mail to the person at the next station who would now be sitting within arm's length. However, when the trainers asked us how to solve the problem of the slow messenger and slow mail progression, our group, in unison, suggested that we needed to fire the messenger (who, of course, was one of our AIG colleagues and, in truth, not really doing a bad job under the circumstances.).

Upon hearing this, one of the Arthur Anderson trainers said, "I've conducted this training for hundreds of companies on three continents. This is the first time I've ever heard people suggesting that we fire the messenger. It's never been done before."

Welcome to the AIG of the 1990s!

CHAPTER 25: FIT TO BE TY'D

Here's a typical example of how some people – although admittedly not all – get hired into the insurance industry. Many of you may think that the insurance industry, with its exacting underwriting protocols and actuarially driven decision making, is populated by precision-oriented bureaucrats who make various decisions only after analyzing reams of relevant data. And you may think that this methodology extends to hiring people. Insurance organizations only offer jobs after doing exacting research, perhaps using artificial intelligence, and ensuring that each candidate is ideal for a particular opening based on a wide variety of finely tuned factors.

Wrong.

That's not how it works. When I'm done laughing at that thought, I will continue writing. (Insert pause)

In fact, it's quite the opposite in many instances. The rolling of dice, the throwing of a dart, or the flipping of a coin might be apt analogies to insurance hiring methods (in many cases, anyway, but certainly not all) (although, see e.g. the Sweatshirt Story earlier in this book.) We will call this next example of insurance industry talent acquisition methods, "The Hiring of Paul Schiavone" (since that's his real name).

Paul had just graduated from New York Law School in 1993 and was promised a job with the District Attorney's Office on Staten Island, where he had grown up. Paul's sole focus in those days, he says, was to become a D.A. and to prosecute criminals. However, due to some type of hiring freeze and/or bureaucratic delay, the D.A.'s Office told Paul he'd have to wait about nine months for his official job offer. With student loan bills poised to roll in, as well as other bills accumulating, Paul was in need of a short-term job.

Cue the insurance opportunity.

Paul's friend Sal Cannestra (son of Stella, RIP, a great woman, and a great insurance professional) got Paul an interview for an internship with a fellow named Ty Sagalow. At the time, Ty was the Chief Underwriting Officer of AIG's National Union subsidiary. Paul had tried to prepare for the interview, but these were pre-Google days and detailed information about companies, and individual executives, wasn't readily available. Nonetheless, Paul showed up eager to snag this short-term internship in order to earn some money before moving on to his dream job of being an Assistant District Attorney on Staten Island. As they say, the best laid plans...

Paul showed up at Ty's office with his resume and some sundry other papers in an impressive-looking leather folio. (Note to aspiring insurance professionals: Impressive-looking folios in an interview generally get you nowhere. In fact, you risk appearing to be a total geek, and we don't need any more of them in the industry.)

Ty started off with some pleasantries, and then quickly got into asking questions of Paul. As Ty progressed with the questions, some solely about insurance, Paul got the sinking feeling that the interview wasn't going well. As the questioning eventually wrapped up, Paul felt fairly certain he wasn't going to get the offer. His suspicions, he believed, were confirmed by Ty's verbal and body language clues.

Just as Paul was gathering his belongings (including, ah hem, his impressive leather folio) to leave, Ty threw out one more random question.

"What do you like to do in your free time?" Ty asked.

"Well," said Paul, "I enjoy performing in theater productions."

"Really," said Ty. "What's your favorite?

"Well," Paul responded, "I'd say 'Fiddler on the Roof.'"

"Hmm, really? That's my favorite, too," Ty said. "Who's your favorite character in Fiddler?"

"Motel Kamzoil, the tailor," said Paul. "I played him in a show not too long ago."

Ty shot back, "Motel is my favorite character, too. I played him in a show in my 20s also, like you. You got the job, when can you start?"

Yes, really, that's how it went.

Paul says that were it not for his shared love of "Fiddler on the Roof" with Ty, he'd probably be working in the Staten Island District Attorney's Office today. Instead, he has had a long and very successful insurance career. Note: He won't have to sing, "If I Were a Rich Man," because, thanks to insurance, he already is!

CHAPTER 26: A GENERAL MIX-UP

While we're on the topic of how people got their first job in the insurance industry, here's one of my favorite stories. It was told to a friend of mine.

A woman went to a college where, during her final year, each senior who was going to be interviewing for jobs (as opposed to, say, going to grad school or into the military) was given five letter-sized pieces of paper that were a unique shade of green. The companies that were coming to campus were each assigned a locked box in the school's Career Counseling Center to receive resumes. Students were told to print their resume on each of the five green pages and to put those in a company's resume-collection box only if the company was one of their top five desired employers. The recipient company would know that the student really wanted to work for that company by virtue of the fact that they were using one of their coveted five green resumes on that company. It was sort of like applying for early acceptance to a college. Or using a silver bullet, but in this case it was green.

The woman who is the focus of our story said that she really wanted to work for General Electric, it was her dream employer. So, she inserted one of her five green resumes into the G.E. box at the Career Counseling Center.

"Seconds after I put the resume in the box," she said, "I took a closer look, and realized that the label above the slot said, 'General Reinsurance,' not General Electric. The boxes were locked, so I couldn't get my green resume back. I had to follow through with the interview. That was 17 years ago, and I'm still working for General Reinsurance today."

CHAPTER 27: TYSON FOODS BIZ TRIP

One of the best business trips I ever took was to visit Tyson Foods in Springdale, Arkansas.

Yes. Really. Arkansas.

It was so fun, in fact, that I agreed with the Courtney Coletti, the underwriter who accompanied me on the trip, that we'd downplay how enjoyable it was when we got back to the office in New York City so other colleagues of ours wouldn't try to muscle in on the trip the following year. This is not a funny story but is meant to illustrate that sometimes in the World of Insurance, enjoyable experiences can crop up where you least expect them.

At the time, in the early 2000s, Tyson Foods had a complex of seven homes on a lake in Northwest Arkansas. These were seven very cool homes, each stocked with all the food you'd want, including Tyson chicken wings (in the freezer, but there were microwaves and ovens), other snacks, and bowls of fruit and candy. Most of the seven houses also had their own pools and very nice grounds. When you think of Arkansas, well, maybe only if you're a snobby Northeasterner, you generally don't think of luxurious homes. But you should. At least in this instance. (Apologies to readers in Arkansas. I'm sure your home is luxurious if you were smart enough to purchase this book. Woo Pig Sooie!)

Courtney and I flew to the Northwest Arkansas Airport in September of 2003. We were there for a renewal meeting on the Tyson Foods Directors & Officers Liability Insurance policy.

Upon arrival at the Tyson compound of houses, we were shown to the main home where our "meetings" would take place. Then we were told we could pick any of the remaining six homes as our accommodation for the two-night stay. The Marsh brokers (Tom Zacharopoulos being among them; I have a self-provided license to use his name anytime I want) were also told to each choose a house for themselves. It was, to say the least, pretty cool.

As is the case occasionally with insurance "meetings," the proceedings were somewhat casual and unstructured. During the course of the two full days that we were there, we went bass fishing (each attendee was on a separate bass boat that was captained by a local expert bass fisherman), had a delicious barbecue of meats that were slow-cooked for 12 hours (while we were out bass fishing), swam in one of the pools, and enjoyed a night of guitar playing and singing by the company's then-CFO.

Everything about the trip was top-notch and enjoyable. But, of course, when Courtney and I returned to our New York office, we complained in an exaggerated manner about how awful the trip to Arkansas was. We were attempting to dissuade anyone else from wanting to go on future Tyson Foods trips.

The lesson from this story: In the future, if you find a colleague complaining excessively about a particular business trip, try to get yourself on that trip the following year, it's probably a fun one!

Chapter 28: Getting More Bang For Your Quarter

Have I mentioned that I enjoy a good practical joke? Admittedly, I even enjoy a BAD practical joke. And it doesn't even have to be that practical; I like impractical jokes, too. Anyway, this one is a doozy, although I've only played it a few times – it's a bit cruel and can cause physical pain to the Victim, and maybe even brain damage. But who am I to say; I'm not a licensed neurologist. Plus, some of these people seemed to have brain damage before I played the trick on them. And while this prank may be a tad bit mean, it does usually elicit uproarious laughter from spectators (and me). On balance, it's my opinion that the audience's enjoyment and laughter is well worth the physical discomfort, and possible concussion/long-term disability, suffered by the Victim.

You know the old saying that a medical procedure where a body is cut into qualifies as "minor surgery" when it's performed on someone else? That philosophy forms the basis of my feelings about this practical joke; it's not cruel when it's done to someone other than me!

By the way, this is another entry that by itself is worth the price of this book. I'm not kidding. Well, I should qualify that statement. It's worth the price of this book – if you possess what I'll refer to as a childlike exuberance. Mature people, especially women, might not find information about this prank all that valuable. Anyway...

The trick is pretty simple. You start by telling the Victim that you can do something that he can't. (I'm purposely using the male pronoun because the trick works better on men.) **Caveat**: The Victim should never be a total stranger; a good friend is preferred because it's always more fun to cause your friends to hurt themselves than a stranger. Plus, a stranger may haul off and punch you in anger when he realizes what happened. There's still that risk with a friend, but it's greatly reduced. As you can see, I'm underwriting this trick for you before you perform it. Please, don't thank me. Oh, and also, the more competitive and high-strung that your friend is, the funnier the trick.

To start, you firmly push a quarter against the middle of your forehead. Hopefully, the quarter will stick. It usually does, especially if your forehead has a small bit of moisture on it (so it's always good to do the trick right after you give a presentation to your boss...). Which reminds me, this trick is performed better, generally, by men since we are sweaty and smelly creatures, as opposed to women who are dry and sweet-smelling. Obviously, I have a Truth-In-Story-Telling policy here.

Next, you lay down the challenge to the Victim (I enjoy capitalizing "Victim," as you've probably guessed) by saying, "I bet you can't knock a quarter off your forehead in less than 10 tries." Then, you turn your head sideways, and <u>gently</u> bang it on a table. As your head hits the table, ideally on the third or fourth bump (so it doesn't look too easy), you wrinkle your forehead and brow, thereby causing the quarter to gently fall onto the table.

Now for the diabolical part (cue the "Exorcist" theme music).

You take the quarter in hand and tell the Victim, again, "I bet you can't do that in fewer than 10 tries."

You might even want to bet a drink, or some small amount of money, just to make it appear more like a legitimate wager. Definitely don't bet a large sum of money on the trick, because the combination of humiliation and significant financial loss will increase the odds of the Victim physically harming you. This is, of course, according to the actuarial tables.

Now here's the sneaky part: You push the quarter very forcefully – so that the Victim can really feel it – into the middle of his forehead. Then, after about five seconds, you pull the quarter away surreptitiously. This is accomplished by gripping the quarter with your fingernails at the top and bottom edges and slowly moving your hand up above the Victim's head. By doing this, the Victim can't see that the quarter is actually in your hand and not still pressed against his forehead. It will still feel to the Victim like the quarter is clinging to his forehead at the spot where you were pushing it in.

The spectators, if you have any, will likely not warn the Victim that the quarter is no longer there. At least I've never seen anyone have the decency to warn anyone. But maybe that's just a function of the moral character of the crowd that I hang out with, I'm not sure.

Usually, what comes next is the Victim hits his head on the table once or twice rather gently. When the Victim sees that the quarter is not falling onto the table, he will ratchet up the level of force with which he's hitting his head on the table. Spectators will start to laugh, which will infuriate the Victim – believing that they are laughing at his ineptitude – which, in turn, causes the Victim to hit his head even harder on the table. I have seen at least one or two people nearly knock themselves unconscious trying to dislodge the quarter that isn't there. All in good fun, of course!

I once did this trick to Peter Levis, a former AIG employee who is long retired from insurance and happily making his fortune in the antiques world. It was on a Friday afternoon in a crowded pub attached to the Lloyd's of London Building. Peter was so zealous in his desire to dislodge the quarter that he started jumping in the air and slamming his head down on the pub's high-top table. Spectators were roaring in laughter. Eventually Peter figured out that there was no quarter on his forehead, but, luckily for me, he was a good sport. In fact, he quickly adopted the trick for his own use and at one point – and I swear this is true – he said, "Larry, you made my life better by showing me that trick."

Now, dear reader, that quote is proof that this gag is money. So go forth and improve the lives of others with this gem!

CHAPTER 29: GOOGLE IT

I'm sure you've heard the phrase, "What goes around, comes around." I'm not 100 percent sure that that observation applies to this story, but it seems appropriate enough. In insurance, sometimes "close enough" will do. In fact, I was recently in an insurance presentation and an actuary said, "Most of these statistics are fairly accurate." Yes, really. In insurance, we usually just need to be "fairly accurate," no sense in knocking ourselves out with precision!

Back in the spring of 2004, just months before Google's August 19, 2004 Initial Public Offering (Yes, you got me, I did have to Google that date.), I was working at ACE Insurance Company when and we received a submission to write the Directors & Officers Liability Insurance for Google's IPO. This entailed covering their liability for alleged wrongful acts arising from the IPO. That seemed, to me anyway, a very risky proposition at the time.

The stock was being offered at a somewhat high price for those days, $85 a share. Besides the high stock price (of course, as of this writing the stock trades well above $85 and has had many splits; hey, I'm an insurance guy, not an investment analyst!), there were a number of factors that made it a risky D&O bet, including the fact that the founders were keeping for themselves some shares with super voting rights. I think they got 10 votes per share. This would help them ensconce themselves in the company's leadership roles for the long haul. There were a number of other factors that militated (whoa, big-word alert!) against writing the account because of the prospect of future lawsuits. After a fair amount of additional research and analysis – yes, it does sometimes occur in insurance – I decided we would decline to quote the account. Declining to quote an account was not commonplace in those days. It was the equivalent of a Taylor Swift concert with plenty of reasonably priced tickets available. You get the idea.

A few days after we declined to quote the account, I received a call from one of the senior executives at ACE, someone who was many levels above me in the org chart. I will conceal his name because he's still prominent, and highly visible, in the insurance industry, and he might not want his name tarnished with a mention in a book like this. Anyway, he called to ask me why we declined to quote Google's IPO. Google's insurance broker at the time, Aon, had called him to complain about the declination. I explained my reasoning. To his, and ACE's, credit, the senior executive supported my decision, and he told Aon that we were sticking by our declination. And, not to toot my own horn – well, OK, maybe a bit – toot, toot! – not too long after the IPO (I can't remember exactly how long, and Googling it was no help, not surprisingly!), Google was hit with one or more securities class actions. And we were not on the account, thank you.

Fast forward now about 10 years. I'm running my own one-man commercial insurance consulting business, and I see an ad on LinkedIn. Google is looking for a new insurance risk manager. On a lark, I sent my resume in. Not long after, I was called for a phone interview. Apparently, it went well, because Google then paid for me to fly from New Jersey to California for in-person interviews. These interviews were not at the company's headquarters in Mountain View, but at similarly cool offices in nearby Sunnyvale, where Google's legal and financial operations were located.

You may not know this, but there have been entire books written about how to apply for a job at Google, and how to shine in the interview. I don't know if these books, which I've never read, talk about interviewing for insurance jobs at Google, but I do know they mention some of the off-beat questions asked of people applying for technology-oriented jobs (some of which pay $3 million or more per year.). Among these questions: "How many golf balls can fit in a standard school bus?" and "How many people worldwide make their living from tuning pianos?"

My guess is, and I don't know this for sure, that Google is more interested in observing your thought process in coming up with an answer, as opposed to actually knowing how many golf balls can fit in a standard (not short) school bus. I don't know the answer to that one, but I'd guess 854,103. I think that's pretty close. Anyway...

The Google offices were super cool, with all sorts of creative and fun features, like swings that hung from the ceilings in hallways, and multi-colored bikes everywhere that anyone could jump on to ride around the sprawling campus. Also, there were snack rooms, nap rooms and conference rooms with unusual names. I was interviewed in the Gary Coleman Conference Room and the Special K Conference Room. Lunch was free to all employees, as were the snacks and soft drinks.

To make a long (and possibly boring, to you) story a bit shorter, I had five interviews, but, ultimately, I was not offered the job. I suspect they knew I turned down a chance to write a layer of their D&O Insurance coverage for their IPO many years earlier, and they were just getting revenge on me by wasting my time with an interview (Hey, I wouldn't put it past them!). Oh well, I got a free trip to California out of it, which wasn't a bad consolation prize. Plus, of course, it provided another story for this book (which will now probably be relegated to the very bottom of Google searches for "Books with Insurance Stories.")

CHAPTER 30: WARREN BUFFETT CAN BE YOUR FRIEND, TOO

The title of this chapter may be a bit misleading – Warren Buffett isn't really my friend. And if you don't already know him, I doubt he'd take you on as a new friend. But there are some worthwhile lessons here.

My first insurance book was published in 2008. I was inspired to write it by the death of a friend at AIG in 2000. His name was Joe Fine, and on the same day in January of 2000 that he was promoted to be the President of AIG's M&A Insurance Group, he died tragically in a car accident at the young age of 34.

I thought at the time that it was a shame that very few insurance people in the future would remember Joe and his accomplishments in the industry. As more people I knew in the insurance industry started retiring and dying, I felt that someone should write a book to capture these legacies in writing for future generations. I looked around and nobody was volunteering, so I figured I'd write the book myself.

I gained quite a few worthwhile insights while writing that first book, titled, *"Claims Made & Reported – A Journey Through D&O, E&O and Other Professional Lines of Insurance."* Please allow me to share a few with you (and if you won't allow me, feel free to skip to the next chapter, I won't be offended.)

When I originally decided to write the book, in 2005, I told myself that I'd write the book whenever I got free time. After the first 18 months, I had exactly 20 typed pages completed. As you'd probably guess, whether you're a writer or not, that's not many pages to show for 18 months of work.

Then, in March of 2007, I took a job that required me to ride a train for one hour each way from my home in Manhattan to Mount Kisco in Westchester County, New York. On the third day of my commute, I decided that I'd close the New York Post (yes, I'm one of the few people who admits to reading it!) and would work on the book on my laptop. Some days I only managed to write a paragraph or two, while on other days I'd get a page or more completed. There's an old saying in England, "How do you eat an elephant? With a teaspoon." A few paragraphs a day can add up quickly, believe it or not, as long as you keep making steady progress with your teaspoon.

After 18 months, I had gone from 20 pages to 376 pages. So, **Lesson #1**: Even just making a little bit of progress toward your goal (whatever it may be, writing a book, painting a portrait, building a shed, etc.) each day will add up. <u>Just keep consistently making progress.</u>

The **Second Lesson**, also illustrated by an old saying, is that you have to have a definite time in mind each day to work on your goal. The old saying here is, "You have to schedule greatness." In the beginning, I was just writing the book "whenever I had free time," which, for most people, including me, is <u>never</u>. There's always something taking up your time. But if you tackle your goal during pre-scheduled times – as I did by virtue of writing each day during my daily commute – you'll make a lot more progress than if you just work at it when "free time" presents itself.

The **Third Lesson**, and this is where my "friend" Warren makes an appearance, is in line with the Zen saying, "Leap and the net shall appear."

I wanted to get some positive comments about the book from senior insurance executives so we could use them in the book's advertising. Almost all proceeds from the book's sales go to charity. This fact made it easier for me, in my mind at least, to encroach upon the time of busy insurance executives to interview them since I wasn't doing it for my own financial gain. In truth, most of the executives were happy to talk to me about old colleagues and to recount stories from their past. And believe it or not, many were more concerned about helping memorialize the legacies of their mentors than they were about getting publicity for themselves.

When it came time to solicit positive comments, I figured I'd go right to the top of the list of Insurance Industry Celebrities, Warren Buffett. Actually, in my mind, Mr. Buffett is tied atop the heap with Maurice R. "Hank" Greenberg, but most Average Joes on The Street would be more familiar with Warren Buffett's name. So, I sent a complimentary copy of the book to Mr. Buffett at Berkshire Hathaway headquarters in Omaha. I got his address from the internet. In my cover note, I asked if he'd read the book and, if he liked it, give me a positive quote or two that we could use in our advertisements for the book. I also told him that almost all the profits went to charity. Mr. Buffett is a renown philanthropist and I figured that this might strike a chord with him.

A few days after I mailed the book, I received a call on my cell phone from Deb Bosanek, Mr. Buffett's wonderful assistant. Side note: Ms. Bosanek was at the State of the Union Address in 2012, where President Obama singled her out as an example of the discrepancies in our national tax system (she apparently paid a higher income tax rate at the time then her billionaire boss). She is, no doubt, a star in her own right.

Anyway, I answered the phone on a beach in Key West, where I was vacationing with my sister and some of her friends. Ms. Bosanek said to me, "Mr. Goanos, this is Deb Bosanek, assistant to Warren Buffett."

"Wow," was all I could say. I was a bit floored. I did not expect this call.

"Mr. Buffett received your book," she said. "Unfortunately, he's too busy to read it, but he thanks you for sending it along."

Needless to say (but I'll say it anyway), I was impressed. Most busy CEOs who receive an unsolicited book in the mail would, I'm sure, just toss it in the round file without a further thought.

But Warren Buffett is no ordinary CEO.

He actually made the effort to have his assistant, Ms. Bosanek, call me to deliver the news, and his thanks, over the phone. Within the next 30 minutes, I had told my sister, her friends and just about anyone else who would listen that, "I just got off the phone with Warren Buffett's assistant." It was the best rejection I had ever received! (And, as a bachelor, I had received many in my day.)

But the story doesn't end there.

Seven months later, on a morning just after the 2009 July 4th holiday weekend, I opened my email to see a "re" line that said, "From Warren Buffett."

Yeah, sure. "Who is trying to BS me?" I thought.

It turns out that it was Mr. Buffett himself. No BS.

Full disclosure, I didn't get Warren's permission to reprint his email here, but something tells me he won't care – especially since all of this book's profits are going to a great charitable cause, the Ryan Pincus Memorial Fund. So here it is (with email addresses omitted):

_____

Dear Larry:

I read your book over the weekend and enjoyed it thoroughly (and *you* didn't think I would open the pages). The section about 9/11 was particularly moving.

I hope our insurance managers got copies as I know they would enjoy it as I did.

Best regards.

Warren

The comment about me not thinking he would read it was in rebuttal to a statement that I had written in the book saying that I could write anything I wanted to about Mr. Buffett because he wouldn't be reading the book. Well, happily, he proved me wrong.

I later learned that Mr. Buffett reads about 500 pages a day to enrich his knowledge of all sorts of issues, not just insurance or business. That's another good tip for anyone, not just young professionals: Read widely and deeply on a regular basis to expand your knowledge. But, of course, you're clearly following that advice already by reading this excellent book!

After reading Mr. Buffett's email, I desperately wanted to get his permission to use part of his comments to help sell the book. An endorsement from Warren Buffett for any kind of product, an insurance or investment book especially, is quite powerful. After consultation with a number of friends, I decided to send him 10 complimentary copies of the book, since he'd written that he hoped his insurance managers would get a copy, and then I'd ask permission to use excerpts of his email in our advertising for the book.

When I sat down to write my response email to him, I kept wavering between addressing him as "Mr. Buffett" or "Warren." After all, I didn't really know him (and still don't), so showing respect by writing "Mr. Buffett" might be in order. But, then again, he referred to me as "Larry," and we were both in the insurance business so, as an industry colleague, "Warren" wouldn't be out of line. Ultimately, I went with "Dear Warren." Yes, a lot of agonizing over a fairly inconsequential issue, I know.

This part will probably not surprise you. Despite having a myriad of demands on his time from all directions, including media interview requests and just the daily hubbub of running Berkshire Hathaway, my now good friend (kidding!) Warren wrote back within an hour of me emailing him on a Monday morning. And, as you might expect, he said he'd be delighted if we used his comments in advertising for the book and that he hoped we sold out every copy and the charities all got a big check.

What a freakin' great guy!

With all that Warren Buffett has going on, it's astounding that he was able to carve out time to respond to an East Coast insurance guy who he had never met. And he was kind enough to offer words of praise also for my second book, "D&O 101." I know this sounds like a thinly veiled attempt to advertise for my first two insurance books (there's a third I won't mention because I'm above that... slightly), but it is sincerely just an effort to praise my pen pal friend Warren for his selfless and generous acts. Of course, there's no shortage of praise in this world for Mr. Buffett, as I mentioned in my third book... oh, wait, sorry, I promised not to reference it.

[Editor's Note: The third insurance book by Mr. Goanos, "Professional Lines Insurance: An Oral History," is available on Amazon.] [**Real Editor's Note**: That previous "Editor's Note" was written by Larry Goanos, not the Editor. The Editor wrote this note to set the record straight. Or maybe it was Larry again, who knows?]

Chapter 31: Magic Beans in the Insurance Industry

At the risk of sounding like a broken record (or, in this modern age, a digital audio recording with a glitch), this story alone is worth the price of this book, especially for younger folks looking to make their mark in the business world. Really, I'm not kidding.

When I was at AIG in the early 2000s, the company owned a very nice golf course in Brewster, New York, called Morefar. It's about 60 miles north of New York City in Putnam County. According to AIG Insurance Lore, the course got its name from businessmen in the Far East who would be invited to play the course when they were in New York to meet with AIG executives. Supposedly – and I kind of doubt this is true, but it's the only origin story I know for the course's name, so I'm going with it – these businessmen, when asked by colleagues in Japan if they were going to golf in New York City, they would reply, "No, more far, more far."

The BS just drips off that one, but we'll buy it in light of this book's inexact – and rather relaxed – standards of fact checking.

Each division within AIG at the time – and there were many – received three or four foursomes each year at Morefar. Management of Morefar purposely kept the number of players low,

I think, to add to its prestige and desirability among the insurance crowd. Also, Morefar had far fewer golf carts than the average course, only about 20, I'd guess, so it couldn't accommodate a high-volume of play anyway.

If you were an AIG manager and you were lucky enough to get a foursome at Morefar, it wouldn't take you more than one or two phone calls to brokers and/or risk managers to fill the slot. Everyone wanted to golf at Morefar, it was THE insurance golf course back in the day (and I think it still is, at least to some extent).

Now, the old profit-driven AIG being the old profit-driven AIG, Morefar, even though it was a "place of serenity," as it said on a sign there, was still a profit center and was expected to make money each season for Mama AIG. Each division within the company that was granted a foursome was charged handsomely for the privilege. So, if someone had to cancel at the last minute and Morefar couldn't charge that division the full freight for the lost foursome opportunity, Morefar would lose money, which, being a part of AIG, was not in its DNA.

Enter The Cancellation List.

The guy who ran Morefar administratively at the time, Al Silverstein (great guy, R.I.P.), had a trusted assistant named Lois. I never met Lois in person, but she became one of the most influential people in my six-and-a-half-year career at AIG. Here's how that happened.

One day in the early spring of 2000, Lois called me because my name had come up as next in line on the l-o-o-o-o-o-o-o-o-o-o-n-g list of AIG profit-center managers who would be asked to take a foursome at the last minute in the event of a cancellation. Lois was trying to fill an empty slot a day before the foursome was scheduled to take place. Her goal was simply to get another group to take the slot, so that Morefar could keep revenue flowing into its coffers. It was all about feeding the machine that was AIG. The entire company needed to help churn out profits. I'm sure shareholders approved of this mentality.

As soon as Lois called me with the cancelation offer, practically before she could get the words out of her mouth, I accepted. The conversation probably went something like this:

Lois: "Hello, Larry, this is Lois from Al Silverstein's office."

Me: "Yes, we'll take it! What time tomorrow?!"

Well, maybe it wasn't exactly like that, but it was close. I was thrilled to have the rare opportunity – with so many other names on the cancellation list – to get a coveted Morefar foursome. I knew better than to hesitate or, worse yet, to decline the offer.

Now here's where I discovered the Magic Beans, akin to those sought by Jack in the tale of "Jack and the Beanstalk." Except these Magic Beans were made of chocolate. But they brought untold riches, just as Jack's had.

The day after we had used that first last-minute foursome, I went to the Duane Reade drugstore by our downtown offices and bought a one-pound bag of …. M&Ms. I sent it to Lois through interoffice mail, along with a note thanking her for offering us the tee time.

LESSON WORTH THE PRICE OF THIS BOOK: Always be nice to administrative assistants, because you never know how they might be able to help you. Plus, it's just a good way to live your life.

About a week later, Lois called again to offer me another cancellation tee time. I thought this was unusual, because I knew there was a long list, and it usually took months, or even a year, before you'd be offered a second last-minute cancelation tee time.

At first, I didn't realize that it was my Magic Beans at work. But I sent Lois another bag of M&Ms after we used that second tee time. Cut to the chase: By the end of that golf season, by my count, our Financial Institutions Group had played Morefar 22 times. Note: I was not greedy, and did not play in all of those foursomes; I was probably only in 19 or 20 of them! It got to the point where our prolific Morefar play was getting noticed. People in other profit centers would see me in the building lobby and say, "Hey, why are you guys in F.I. getting so many Morefar tee times?" I, of course, shrugged in feigned ignorance and said something like, "Just luck, I guess."

As it turned out, M&Ms might well have stood for More Morefar.

This very valuable secret, dear readers, is now known to you. It's wise to go out of your way to always treat administrative/executive assistants well. It may pay valuable dividends in the long run. And even if it doesn't, it's the right thing to do. Now go forth and prosper with this powerful knowledge!

CHAPTER 32: PAUL SULT

This is the only chapter in this book that profiles just a single person. Paul Sult was a legend in the Professional Lines Insurance Industry. They don't make them like Paul anymore (although, that might be a good thing; Paul was a handful from what I gather!)

Paul W. Sult II was a prolific professional lines insurance innovator during an illustrious career that spanned almost 40 years. When I first contacted Paul by phone in 2008, he was 81 years young and still full of wit and wisdom (not to mention piss and vinegar). I called him many times to interview him for "Claims Made and Reported," my first insurance book, and he started off the conversation the same way each time we spoke.

"Larry, I'm 81 years old. You know what my secret is? I have a great doctor." Then there would be about a three-second pause, and he'd yell, "And his name is Jack Daniels!" Paul would then guffaw loudly every time he said it, which, as noted, was at the beginning of each of our many calls. It was as if he were hearing his own joke for the first time (but then again, I can't fault him since I've been accused of laughing at my own jokes too.).

Paul told me he was drawn to insurance genetically; his father owned the Firemen's & Mechanics' Insurance Company in Fort Wayne, Indiana.

"The Indiana state legislature chartered four or five insurance companies way back in 1850," he explained, "Firemen's & Mechanics' was one of them. It was originally chartered in Madison, Indiana, to insure boats on the Ohio River."

Paul, who was prevented from serving in the military by a case of childhood polio that disabled his right ear drum (although, upon further reflection, I'm wondering if his eardrum became disabled from all the loud guffawing that he did...), started his insurance career with the family business in 1945. He began on the bottom rung, working in the Mail and Supply Department of Firemen's & Mechanics'. In 1948, he transferred into the Underwriting Department as a trainee. While working full time, he attended company-sponsored insurance classes for three years. It wasn't until 1958 that Paul got into Professional Lines Insurance when he moved to Allentown, PA, to work for the Stuyvesant Insurance Company.

In 1959, while a department manager at Stuyvesant, Paul wrote the first group medical malpractice insurance policy in the United States for the Los Angeles County Medical Society.

Paul moved to Chicago in 1963 to become a field rep with wholesale brokerage Stewart Smith Mid-America, a unit of London-based Stewart Smith. "I started out as a 'Field Man,'" he recalled, "I traveled throughout the Midwest telling agents and brokers about various Stewart Smith products."

Paul's first of many significant insurance innovations occurred in 1968. Paul was heading out to lunch in Chicago when his boss at Stewart Smith, Harold Frederick, handed him a letter. It was from Charles Peters, an employee of NP Dodge, a real estate brokerage in Omaha. Mr. Peters was about to serve on the Omaha School Board and a friend had asked him if he had insurance to cover school board-related liabilities. Mr. Peters didn't have such coverage, so he wrote to Stewart Smith in Chicago inquiring about the possibility of obtaining a policy.

When Paul's boss handed him the letter, Paul was anxious to strap on the feedbag as he headed out to lunch, so he took a quick look at the letter and after declaring that there was no such coverage available, he balled it up and threw it into the trash on his way out the door.

"Later, on my second martini at lunch," Paul told me, "I realized that there might be a new product there." When Paul returned to his office, he fished the letter out of the garbage and contacted Mr. Peters. Paul drafted the industry's first School Board Members' E&O policy by himself, in longhand, while lying in a hospital bed recovering from colitis. He convinced some Lloyd's of London syndicates to take on this new exposure, but regulatory hurdles prevented him from using Lloyd's paper directly as the issuing insurance carrier. Paul found a company in Los Angeles, Pacific Indemnity, that was willing to front the product, but only if the lion's share of the exposure was reinsured to a Lloyd's syndicate.

"After one year, due to a management change, Pacific Indemnity got cold feet," Paul remembered, "So CNA agreed to write it (no doubt convinced by Paul's silver tongue.). We went to conventions, put up booths and did a lot of marketing. There were 12,000 school districts in the U.S. in those days and before long we were insuring about 8,000 of them."

Paul's School Board Members' E&O product was such a success that he decided the concept could work elsewhere. "I bought a book that listed all of the colleges in the United States and wrote letters asking if they would be interested in insurance coverage for their trustees and other university leaders," he explained. Paul tailored the School Board Members' E&O form to college and university officials, including trustees and members of Boards of Regents, and was soon selling another new product. In the 1970s, he continued the evolution of his School Board Members' E&O product by introducing Public Officials' Liability insurance to cover people serving in roles such as mayors and police officers.

Paul's next innovation came in response to the growing number of federal laws regulating fair employment practices in the late 1960s and beyond. He drafted a form, referred to as FEPL (Federal Employment Practices Liability), to cover companies' liabilities for employment-related violations. Paul approached CNA to write this new product. He had London reinsurance all lined up, a familiar arrangement by now, but CNA turned him down. The carrier's in-house lawyers believed a product insuring against potentially intentional acts of employment discrimination, harassment and the like would contravene public policy. He approached his old employer, Stuyvesant Insurance Company, but it, too, declined to write the coverage. Paul was ahead of his time in developing Employment Practices Liability (EPL) insurance, a coverage routinely sold today. Unfortunately, he never found an American carrier willing to assume the exposure, although it would eventually become a very popular product.

Al Wayne, chairman and founder of Chicago insurance brokerage Alexander J. Wayne & Associates, has a lot of fond memories of working with Paul at Stewart Smith Mid-America.

One of his favorites starts with a walk back to the office in Chicago with Paul and a group of co-workers after a celebratory lunch for a colleague who had been promoted. There had been plenty of toasts and everyone was feeling good. The group passed a car dealership displaying a cedar brown Rolls Royce Silver Shadow in its showroom window.

"It was probably the only new Rolls for sale in Chicago," Al recalls. Paul announced that he needed a new company car and led the men inside for a closer look at the Rolls. Paul asked an eager young salesman if he could take the car for a test ride, but the salesman refused, saying his boss would fire him. Al, thinking he was playing along with the game, asked the car's price and was told $89,000 – a princely sum for a car in the early 1970s. His broker instincts took over, and Al negotiated the number down to

$78,000. Paul was still busy kicking the tires and looking under the hood when Al broke the news that he had managed to carve $11,000 off the price. Al hoped that this would impress his boss before they headed outside to get a cab back to the office. Much to Al's surprise, Paul called Stewart Smith Mid-America's CFO and told him to get down to the Rolls dealership ASAP with a check for $78,000. Within half an hour, Al recalls, the men were driving back to the office in Paul's new Rolls Royce.

Paul's story proves that if you become a big-time producer of revenue in the insurance industry, the sky is the limit. Also, there is plenty of room in insurance for innovators like Paul Sult who think outside the box. Creativity is not only encouraged, but rewarded, too.

Paul and his lovely wife, the former Winifred Dean, spent many years of blissful retirement in North Carolina before Paul's passing in 2010.

CHAPTER 33: NOT THE BEST MAN FOR THE JOB

One of the many benefits of working in the commercial insurance industry is that you meet, and befriend, people from all over the globe. While working at Marsh in San Francisco in the late 1990s, I had the good fortune of meeting Tim Mitchell. Tim, a native of England, worked in our Global Broking Group (those were the people who dealt directly with underwriters to get deals done), and I was in FINPRO on the client side, the group that dealt directly with clients (some would say the better-looking and smarter people worked in FINPRO; well, if you consider me to be "some people!").

Tim was (and still is) a great guy. He eventually moved back to London and got engaged to the lovely and talented Tara Falk, co-founder (with James Kalbassi) of the highly successful (and I don't say that lightly) insurance brokerage Paragon International Insurance Brokers Ltd.

I also left San Francisco, in late 1998, to return to New York. I received a call from Tim in early 2004. I remember the call clearly. I was at work in my office at ACE Insurance at 140 Broadway in downtown Manhattan.

"Larry," he said, "You're going to be receiving an invitation to my wedding soon. Tara and I are getting married in the Beaujolais wine region of France in June. In England, we have a tradition where one of the groom's mates gives a speech at the reception, it's mostly about the groom. It's not just a short toast like in America, but a full-on speech. My two best mates are not really great orators, and I'd like you to give the speech, if you would."

Before he was done asking, I had already said, "Yes, I'll do it!"

Then he explained that the purpose of the speech is to poke good-natured fun at the groom. "The only thing off-limits," he said, "Is my first marriage. And you can't insult Tara in any way."

I was fine with those ground rules in exchange for getting to give a speech at a wedding reception in France. In case you haven't picked up on it yet, I'm a bit of a ham (and might be available to give a speech at your wedding; just ask!)

Tim then went on to give me the phone numbers of his two best friends in London. He told me I should call them to get some good stories I could use for the speech.

A lesson that I knew before this incident in 2004, one that was recently reinforced while I was writing this book and had solicited interesting stories from my 4,000+ LinkedIn contacts (and received exactly one response), is that when asked to provide an interesting or funny story or joke on the spot, most people freeze up and can't respond. Even with a lot of time to reflect upon it, most people can't come up with great stories, which might be why this is the only book of insurance stories that you've ever read. Not that they are necessarily great, but hey, I'm trying!

I called the first of Tim's two best friends and he said, "Uh, uh, oh, uh, I can't think of anything right now. Call me back in two weeks." Two weeks seemed like an inordinately long time to allow one to think up a single funny story, so I wrote him off as someone who wouldn't be able to provide any material.

I got Tim's second friend on the line, and he, too, was at a loss.

"Don't you have anything?" I asked. "Think back, was Tim ever arrested? Did he throw up at a bar? Did he ever get caught with a prostitute? Anything interesting, anything at all."

"No, no, nothing like that," said Friend #2. Then, after a bit of a pause, he piped up: "Wait, wait, I have something. Tim is really bad at math!"

Umm, yeah, great, I thought. This guy clearly wasn't writing material for Ricky Gervais.

"That's not really very funny," I said, "I don't think that's a great basis for a story as part of the speech at the reception."

"But you don't understand," said Friend #2, very enthusiastically, "His dad was a math teacher!"

Cue the guffaws. Not.

"Uh, OK, I'll try to work with that, thanks," I said as I hung up, knowing that I'd need to write 100 percent of this speech myself, with no help from Tim's childhood friends.

As most people in my shoes would do, even though I had three- or four-months advanced notice of my need to write this speech – the wedding was in June 2004 – I waited until the last minute to draft it, during the flight over to London. I just had a feeling that inspiration would hit me at some point. It was blind faith, of course.

I did find my inspiration during the trip over, in the form of some postcards I saw of celebrities' faces in a bookstore at JFK Airport before our plane departed. I was traveling with Stefano Minale, a friend of Tim's and mine who has been a long-time HCC Claims Executive. I purchased five or six of these postcards and decided to write fictitious messages of support for the marriage of Tim and Tara as if they were coming from those celebrities depicted on the postcards. Among the postcard images were Queen Elizabeth, Harry Potter and then-U.S. President George W. Bush (the son, for those of you who can't keep the middle initials straight). More on the speech shortly, keep reading!

Tim had told me I'd have to stop in London before heading to France in order to pick up my "morning suit." Being an American (although lacking a gun or a pickup truck), I had no idea what a "morning suit" was. Turns out, it's what we'd call a "tuxedo" here in the good ole U.S. of A. Another Google search informed me that it's called a "morning suit" in England because English gentlemen in the 19th century would ride their horses in the morning wearing a "cutaway front, single-breasted morning coat." More bonus knowledge for reading this book!

The day after we landed in London, Stefano and I went to the haberdashery (a genuine olde-tyme word!) where I was to pick up my morning suit. Irreverent Side Note: Given that I was a confirmed bachelor at the time, and had a dim view of marriage, I legitimately thought at first that it might actually be a "mourning suit," as in mourning the end of one's bachelorhood.

At the store, a very nice young lady assisted me by procuring the suit from the back room of the store and helping me try on the jacket. She knew I was attending the Mitchell/Falk wedding in France.

"I don't have a date," I said, "Would you like to come with me to the wedding?"

Her immediate response: "No, no, sorry, Tim warned me about you!"

Wow. I guess that was how it was going to be. Note: I would not really have taken her, but I thought it would be amusing to ask and, maybe, the comment might even make it into a book 20 years later.

Stefano and I took a flight from London to Lyon's Saint-Exupery International Airport. We had planned on renting a car and driving to the quaint French farmhouse bed-and-breakfast that would serve as our quarters during the wedding weekend. Tim and Tara had made the reservations for us at the farmhouse. I'm generally a hater of bed-and-breakfast establishments; I'd much rather stay at a Hyatt or Marriott or other chain hotel, but that wasn't an option. Neither of us spoke French, but we were hoping that wouldn't be an impediment to reaching our rural farmhouse destination. This was, of course, before Google Maps or other apps that could guide us. However, Lady Luck smiled upon us that day, rendering our lack of French language skills irrelevant.

As everyone stood up after the plane stopped taxiing in Lyon, Stefano said to me, "Larry, I think that guy over there just said your name."

I looked over and saw Giles Stockton, a revered Lloyd's underwriter who I knew through the insurance industry (again, you can make friends everywhere when you work in insurance, it's a great benefit of being in the industry!) Giles was a U.K. citizen, but his mother had been born and raised in France, and he spoke French impeccably, having spent many childhood summers in the country. After a brief exchange, Giles offered to drive us to the farmhouse, where he was also staying. Thus, we didn't need a rental car and our inability to read French road signs would not be a problem. Giles had saved the day.

When we got to the farmhouse, the hosts showed us each to our separate rooms and gave us the lay of the land regarding breakfast, etc. It was a large, rustic farmhouse, probably as you are picturing it in your mind from various movies, and it was set in the middle of acres and acres of grapevines. The nearest neighbor was probably a mile away or more. Scratch that, a kilometer away or more.

I am not an interior decorator and have no interior design skills or acumen (as my wife will gladly tell you). The décor of my room seemed to me to be that of a stereotypical French farmhouse – even though this was the first French farmhouse that I'd been in; nonetheless, I had a clear idea of what would be stereotypical! There were French-style paintings on the walls (again, I had no real idea), various knick-knack decorations, and a box on the dresser, under a painting of the French countryside, which said "Hermes" on it. Given that Hermes is a French company, I just assumed the box was part of the French décor. A bit of overkill in my opinion, but whatevs.

The next day, we all got into our clothes for the wedding, and Giles drove us to the church, a magnificent structure at the top of a hill overlooking nine vineyards in the Beaujolais Wine Region. It was a glorious Saturday morning, replete with brilliant sunshine and the sound of chirping birds filling the deep-blue sky. It was like something you'd see in a Disney film. As the 110 or so guests filed into the church, I was handed a program. To my great surprise – shock even – the program listed me as the "Best Man." I was probably naïve to not realize it, but by virtue of the fact I was to give the main speech at the reception, I was the official Best Man. I can't say for sure, but I'd bet that it's rare for a guy to show up at a wedding and not discover until he's in the church and reading the program that he is that wedding's Best Man. It was certainly a first for me.

The next shock was more embarrassing for me, a "dawn breaks on Marblehead/duh" type of moment. I looked at the other four or so groomsmen, and they were all wearing light blue Hermes ties. My morning suit had come with a standard gray tie, which looked rather pedestrian in comparison to the other groomsmen. Tim saw me shortly after I arrived at the church and walked over to me to ask, "Where's your tie?"

"I'm wearing it," I replied, "This is the tie that I got in London with the morning suit."

"Wasn't there a Hermes box on the dresser in your room when you arrived yesterday? That's where your light blue Hermes tie was," he said.

"Oh s***," I replied, not caring about cursing in church. "I thought that box was part of the room décor, I didn't dare open it. I didn't want to get in trouble!" I was already proving myself unworthy of being the Best Man and the ceremony hadn't even started.

More about the Hermes tie shortly, stay tuned.

The ceremony was well done and extremely moving. At one point, when organ music was needed, Giles Stockton, our fluent-in-French driver and insurance legend, got up from his seat, walked over to the organ and sat down to play a stunning rendition of some song I'm not cultured enough to know. He played the song flawlessly and it was amazing. Giles is a genuine Renaissance Man! I wondered if he was going to whip up a gourmet meal for the reception and possibly cure cancer while he was at it. He has been retired from insurance for a while now, but I'm sure he's still impressing people on a regular basis.

After the wedding ceremony, all of the guests walked through a long tunnel at a nearby winery, a dark passage lit by a trail of candles, until we emerged into a large room that contained wine casks that were each the size of an SUV. This room, too, was lit by a multitude of candles and some other low lights and was just super cool. There was one long table as I recall (possibly two; it was 20 years ago, after all), where all 110 or so guests sat next to each other. After some prefatory remarks from the parents and, possibly others (again 20 years ago), it was time for me to deliver the speech. Earlier in day, Tim had said to me, "Tara is a bit nervous about your speech. If it's not going well, you can just end it quickly and sit down, no need to drag it out."

"Sorry Tim," I said, "I have it written, and I have to go through with the whole thing. Don't worry, it will be fine." I didn't really know if it would be fine – this was my first speech at a European wedding after all – but I couldn't show any weakness at this point. It was go time!

I didn't save a written version of the speech (it may have been videotaped, I'm not sure), but I do recall, verbatim, the last segment. Most of the speech was funny – in my opinion – and even though the speech is intended to take shots at the groom, I went fairly easy on Tim … until the end.

After having shown various postcards with celebrities' faces on them and reading the messages that I had written on back, including one postcard of Harry Potter, who some people thought looked like Tim (sorry Tim), I came to the last one, which contained a likeness of George W. Bush. And here's what I said:

"This message comes to us today from the American President, George W. Bush. President Bush couldn't be here today, but he asked me to convey this message to Tim. 'I am declaring Saturday, June 5th, 2004, to be Tim Mitchell Day in America. Tim as an individual is the single largest trading partner of the American pharmaceutical industry, and we appreciate his business. Tim's enormous purchases of Viagra have contributed greatly to the American economy, and we appreciate it. So, to Tim, I say, thanks for the wanks, from the Yanks!"

The crowd mostly loved it and laughed heartily…except for an elderly woman who was seated near Stefano. He later told me she audibly gasped and said, "Did he just say wanks?!" Luckily, she didn't pass out. Oh well, you can't please everyone.

The speech was mostly well received overall. So much so, in fact, that another insurance industry guest, a guy in his early 30s, offered to pay to fly me over to London if I'd give the speech as his wedding in a few months. I was tempted, but I declined. And I am shielding that individual's identity, in case he now, in retrospect, regrets making that offer.

The reception matched the awesomeness of the ceremony; it was off-the-charts fun. One of the insurance industry's most colorful and fun characters was there, Tommy Gamble (rest in peace; Tommy passed away in 2022). He always brought the party with him, and the Mitchell/Falk Reception was no exception. Tommy had rented a room in an old castle (he may have even rented the entire castle, I can't remember) and made the weekend even more fun. He was certainly one-of-a-kind.

And, thankfully, my use of the word "wanks" in the speech didn't get me banned from future weddings (none that I know of, anyway) and provided an amusing anecdote for future telling.

Now, as promised, a revelation about that Hermes tie, which you probably forgot about at this point, I'm sure.

Tim and Tara: If you are reading this book, please jump to the next section; I've never told you this and was hoping you'd never find out, but I feel I need to include it here to make this story whole, and to be intellectually honest with our dear readers.

I brought the tie back with me to New York City, where I lived at the time. Those who know me know I'm not a "clothes horse," or a "big fashion guy" (picture Chris Farley using his fingers to make air quotes around those two phrases). I was somewhat reluctant to wear the tie after I learned how expensive it was – much more costly than any tie that I had ever purchased for myself.

A quote about expensive ties that resonates with me was said by my friend Joe O'Neill (a now-retired Boston lawyer; also, a great guy): "Every tie is just a meatball sub away from extinction." I couldn't bear the thought of spilling something on that exquisite – and expensive – tie and ruining it. So, I kept it safely stored in my closet, hidden away from subs, pizza, pasta and culinary threats of all kinds which might bring about its demise. For those who don't know, once a tie is stained, you can't really save it. Even dry cleaning doesn't do the trick.

One of my colleagues at the time at insurance brokerage Marsh, Devin Beresheim, was, and still is, a clothes horse and a fashionable dresser. He had many Hermes ties in his collection at the time. This is back when men wore ties to work daily, of course. I mentioned to Devin that I, too, had a high-end Hermes tie; he wasn't the only one. I told him that it was light blue, and that Tim and Tara had given it to me as a gift, but I was afraid to wear it because I didn't want to ruin it.

"I'll tell you what," he said, "I'll buy the tie off of you for $75, and I'll treat you to a sushi lunch as well. What do you say?"

"Deal," I said without hesitation. Although I added a condition, "You can never tell anyone, especially Tim and Tara, that I sold you this tie." He agreed, although I guess he's now free of that condition since I'm ratting myself out publicly. I contacted Devin recently to get his permission to use his name in this story and he happily reported that he still has the light-blue Hermes tie. It has avoided meatball subs and all other methods of ruination to this day.

Later that year, when I was dating an insurance industry colleague, I made the mistake of telling her that I had once owned a Hermes tie, but that I sold it to Devin. Her response: "Devin has class and good fashion sense. I should probably be dating him." Note ladies: Devin was at the time, and still is, happily married, so back off!

CHAPTER 34: THE RIGHT MAN FOR THE OFFICE

On August day in the year 2000 or so, when I was working at AIG, my sister Maria called to tell me that she was in Manhattan with her friend Gail, and they wanted to swing by 175 Water Street to see my office in an hour or so since they had never been. I agreed.

My office was OK, nothing to be embarrassed about, but it paled in comparison to an office I had seen a few days earlier on one of the top floors of our building. That sprawling office, about six or eight times larger than mine, had a panoramic view of the East River and Brooklyn. It's inhabitant, John Doyle, had at one time been roughly on the same level as me at AIG subsidiary National Union, but he had now ascended way up the ranks to the prestigious role of being president of a large subsidiary of the company.

However, besides being super smart and super successful, John was also a nice guy (and still is today, in his role as CEO of Marsh). So, I decided to play a trick on my sister and her friend.

I called John and asked if I could sit in his office and have my assistant direct my sister and Gail to his office so that I could pretend, for a bit anyway, that it was mine. He graciously agreed, but he said, "I have some work to do here at my computer, I can't just leave the office right now."

"That's OK," I said, "I can work around that."

I went upstairs to John's office a few minutes before my sister and Gail were to arrive. When they did, my assistant told the security guard to send them upstairs to John Doyle's floor.

When they stepped off the elevator, I greeted them and brought them into John's palatial suite. He was busy focused on what he was doing on the computer. Here's where I probably went a bit overboard.

"Don't be distracted by him," I said, pointing over to John. "That's the I.T. guy and he's fixing my computer." John didn't flinch.

"Wow, this is a gigantic office," my sister Maria said. Continuing with my over-the-top (and somewhat ungrateful) behavior, I said to John, "Keep working hard my man and maybe this will be your office someday."

Without missing a beat, John looked up from the computer and said to my sister and her friend Gail, "Actually, this used to be my office, now I have a much bigger one."

Touché!

That was pretty good quick thinking by John. And, of course, at that point I had to confess to the truth before thanking John and bringing my visitors down to my much more modest work digs. But to me, this story illustrates the fact that even the people at the highest level of the industry – most of them anyway – still maintain a down-to-earth and fun attitude.

CHAPTER 35: THE ROLLS ROYCE OF BUSINESS MEETINGS

This story took place more recently than any other in this book. It happened in October 2023, when I was working at large wholesale brokerage Amwins as a full-time outside consultant. And there's a weird twist to it, which I will share before I get to the main part of the story, since it's my book and I can pretty much write whatever I want (within reason, of course; the publisher does employ editors and censors!).

First, the tangential part: In August 2023, an ad randomly popped up on my Facebook feed for a "Halloween Psychic Fair" that was taking place at the end of October in Wurtsboro, New York. My wife and I are interested in that sort of thing, so I checked Google Maps to see where Wurtsboro, a town I had never heard of, was located in relation to our house at the Jersey Shore.

Wurtsboro, it turned out, was about a two-and-a-half-hour drive from our house. While the psychic fair interested me, I felt that such a long drive was out of the question. I knew my wife would not be up for it, so I dismissed the idea.

Fast forward two months. I got invited to an event hosted by Arch Insurance at the Monticello Motor Club in Monticello, New York.

Shout out here to Anna Kodryanu and Mark Lange, they are excellent hosts. Note: Since that previous sentence was written, Anna departed Arch for Westfield Specialty. A great thing about insurance is that there is a lot of mobility, especially after you gain some work experience, keep that in mind kids.

I've never had this confirmed, but since I was invited about two weeks before the event, I'm pretty sure that I was a last-minute fill-in for an Amwins colleague who canceled. Whoever they are, I thank them!

Another lesson: You can't be too proud in the insurance industry when you're offered opportunities for boondoggles... Err, I mean opportunities for business development!

About two hours into the drive to Monticello, I saw a sign on the freeway for an exit that said, "Wurtsboro – 6 Miles."

What were the freakin' odds?

I had never heard of Wurtsboro in my life, and now was about to drive past it on my way to a work event. I was running uncharacteristically early, so, of course, I turned off the freeway and followed the signs to Wurtsboro.

I'm guessing that at least a few people reading this book are familiar with Wurtsboro. It's a perfectly nice little town, sort of a typical Upstate New York hamlet. The main drag is a quaint little stretch about a half mile long, based upon my highly unreliable sense of direction and geography. As I drove along looking at all the stores, I eventually passed a store named, "The Crystal Connection." I decided to park and check it out.

I walked into this fairly large, by Main Street standards anyway, store. I later learned the building was formerly a Methodist Church. I saw a clerk behind one of many counters. This nice woman was probably in her late 30s and had the friendly demeanor of most Upstate New Yorkers (in my experience, anyway).

"I'm here for a really weird reason," I said. "I saw a pop-up ad on Facebook a few months ago about a Psychic Fair in this town. I had never heard of Wurtsboro. And now, on my way to a work event from the Jersey Shore where I live, I saw the sign for Wurtsboro, so I made a detour here. I assume this store participates in the Psychic Fair, correct?"

The woman's reply: "This store is where the Psychic Fair takes place. It's all in here."

Whoa.... weird... coincidence. Now on to the rest of the story.

The first day/night of the Arch racing event consisted of a few meetings to discuss how Amwins and Arch could do more business together in mutually beneficial ways, and then there was a dinner in one of the restaurants at the casino/hotel complex where we were all staying.

The next morning, we drove to the nearby Monticello Motor Club for a day of driving an assortment of high-performance vehicles in a variety of settings. At first blush, as an insurance guy, I thought it was a fairly risky corporate outing – amateurs driving high-performance cars at high speeds. But the instructors at the club assured us that it was perfectly safe, as long as we did what they told us, including not look at our phones while driving at high speeds (insert your own version of "duh" here; but I guess they say it for a reason, some people must do it...)

There was a drag-racing session to start the day, followed by driving at high speeds on an asphalt oval, and then racing on dirt tracks while maneuvering at high speeds around traffic cones. Among the car brands that we drove were BMW, Aston Martin, Rolls Royce and Porsche. Hyundai and Kia were noticeably absent. They clearly weren't skimping on quality with the cars. And our drives were timed, so it was a competitive environment, but nonetheless enjoyable.

Until an episode just after lunch.

Well, for some people it wasn't enjoyable. For me, I must admit, it was.

After a nice buffet lunch in one of the club's dining rooms, people started to wander outside to await the next driving activity. Just outside the dining room, there were a number of high-end cars parked randomly. I noticed a group of about seven or eight men (yes, all men), including some from Amwins, Arch and one or two staff members of the Monticello Motor Club. They were admiring a $450,000 Rolls Royce that we had driven earlier in the day.

One of the men said, "I have to see the engine on a $450,000 Rolls Royce," and he began searching for the latch to open the hood. He was having difficult, and soon five or six other men joined him in the quest up by the car's grill to find the latch to open the hood. Someone had discovered the first step in opening the hood – whatever they did caused it to open about 2 inches – but it still wouldn't open all the way.

I know this will be hard to believe, but seven or eight men, including at least one employee of the Monticello Motor Club, could not figure out how to open the hood of this Rolls Royce. They were all crouched down looking at various areas of the car's grill, when I said, "Maybe there's a release button on the driver's side of the car's dashboard."

With that, I opened the car's driver-side door and began scanning the dashboard and lower areas of the driver's side for some type of release button or latch.

WARNING: DO NOT TRY THIS AT HOME!

After what was admittedly only about five seconds or so, I was hit with devilish inspiration. To quote old-tyme comedian Flip Wilson (some of you are probably old enough to remember him), "The devil made me do it."

I cannot tell you what compelled me to do this, but without thinking, as seven or eight guys had their heads and faces right up against the car's grill in search of the hood release latch, I pressed the car's horn. Hard.

WAAAAAAAAAAAA! it wailed.

It was loud. Some might say ear-piercing. Especially if your face was right up against the grill, like the seven or eight guys trying to figure out how to open the hood.

As the group all recoiled in unison and leapt back from the car, I stepped out from behind the driver's side door, laughing like a hyena on ecstasy (I've never seen a hyena on ecstasy, but I'm guessing here).

My Amwins colleague Dave Lewison later said to me, "I thought at first that we had set off some type of alarm on the car, but when you emerged from behind the driver's door laughing, I knew that you had blown the horn. I was only mad because had I known you were going to do that, I would've lured more people close to the grill."

Ah, good, clean fun among mature insurance professionals – blowing a car horn directly in the face of a group of colleagues. You can't beat it!

And later, another one of my Amwins colleagues, Jeff McNatt, said to me, "I thought I was going to have to fight that Motor Club employee for you, he was really mad. He wanted to beat you up."

One more valuable lesson from the Insurance World: It's good to work with colleagues who have your back!

CHAPTER 36: HIS RATING DIDN'T GET A LYFT

Once a person progresses a bit in their insurance career, they get to participate in a lot of fun things, such as golf and other sporting event outings, conferences at posh resorts and dinners at upscale restaurants. And many of these events become fond memories when looking back over one's insurance career.

This story isn't exactly one of those.

Well, it's memorable, but not in a fond way. Oh well, they can't all be winners.

In March 2022, I attended an insurance claims conference at the JW Marriott Desert Springs Resort & Spa in Palm Desert, California. My stepson Eric, who works for Chubb, accompanied me. It was his first insurance conference. Also at the conference were my friend Stefano Minale, Chief Claims Officer of Tokio Marine HCC, and his son Stef, who also worked for TMHCC at the time but has since moved on to another company. Clive, a Claims manager in TM HCC's London office was also there, along with another friend of mine, the managing partner of a large insurance defense law firm who asked that I not use his name in this story (apparently, he has good judgment). We'll just call him MPLF (Managing Partner Large Law Firm). MPLLF, Stefano and I spoke on a panel together.

As you may recall, in March of 2022, the COVID-19 pandemic was still gripping America. Many people, but not all, wore masks and had been vaccinated.

On the Wednesday night of the conference, MPLLF generously invited Stefano, Clive, Stef, Eric and me to a dinner at a steakhouse about a 15-minute ride from the JW Marriott where we were all staying. We took two Ubers to the restaurant.

When the meal concluded, close to midnight, we tried to arrange for two Ubers to return us to the hotel. Apparently because of the conference, Ubers were in high demand on that Wednesday night, even at midnight. We could only book one Uber, no others were available. We also tried the local cab companies, but no luck.

Finally, MPLLF managed to reserve a Lyft using his phone's app.

The Uber and the Lyft cars arrived in front of the steakhouse contemporaneously. Stefano and his son Stef and my stepson Eric were getting into the Uber that Stef had ordered when MPLLF, Clive and I tried to enter the Lyft. It wasn't a very large car, and it seemed to make more sense for me to ride in the front than to squish three adults (Note: I qualify as an "adult" in this situation) into the back seat.

When I opened the front passenger door of the Lyft, I saw a notebook and some loose papers on the seat.

"We're not supposed to let anyone ride in the front," the driver loudly chirped at me, "Company policy." He was unmistakenly irritated that I would even think about riding in front.

I replied, "OK," and I turned and yelled to Stefano, about 10 yards away in the Uber, "Hey Stef, this guy won't let me ride in the front, do you guys have room?"

As soon as I my sentence was finished, the Lyft driver exploded.

"I didn't say that you couldn't ride in the front, I said it's against company policy!" And with that, his right arm violently swept the notebook and papers off the seat and onto the floor.

Whoa.

At this point, I was a bit hesitant to get into the Lyft, but I didn't have much choice. The Uber was full and there were no other car services available at midnight on a Wednesday in Palm Springs.

I took my seat in the front and closed the door, and the Lyft driver began to drive. I was trying to figure out why he was so angry, and the only thing I could think of was that he didn't want three passengers in his car with COVID still raging (I didn't think of the possibility that he had two dead bodies in the trunk until later.) Trying to appease him, I made a tactical error.

"Just so you know, we've all been vaccinated," I said.

"IT DOESN'T MATTER IF YOU'VE BEEN VACCINATED, YOU CAN STILL PASS THE VIRUS TO SOMEONE!" He yelled with an extreme ferocity that can't be approximated even by the use of all capital letters. Think along the lines of 12,000-point font and you'll get the idea. Oh, and bold-faced.

Foolishly thinking that there might be another way to somehow placate the madman driver, who I now thought was possibly the Unabomber's son, I said, "Well, none of us have COVID now, and none of us have had it ever."

Another wrong move.

"IT DOESN'T MATTER IF YOU DON'T HAVE COVID, YOU CAN STILL PASS IT ON TO SOMEONE ELSE!" he screamed. Very loudly.

Now, at this point, you'd think that I'd just clam up, especially with the dearth of cars available to give me a ride back to the hotel should the Lyft driver decide that he had experienced enough of my COVID observations and chose to kick me out of his car.

But, of course, I didn't take that wise, clam-up route. However, if I had, this story wouldn't be in this book, so that's some consolation for me.

Instead, I quickly retorted, without really thinking about the potential consequences, "I'm sorry, where did you say that you got your degree in Virology?"

Mt. Vesuvius eruption number three quickly ensued.

"YOU DON'T NEED A DEGREE IN VIROLOGY TO KNOW THAT!" he screamed with such vigor that I was surprised the car windows didn't shatter.

Luckily, I caught on pretty quickly. It only takes three eardrum-popping level screams for me to understand the gravity of the situation. I did not want to walk the five miles back to the hotel after midnight on a Wednesday, so I didn't say a word for the rest of the ride.

Now here's the funny part – to me anyway. As you might know, rideshare drivers don't only receive ratings from passengers, they also get to rate the passengers so that other drivers will know if a passenger represents a desirable fare or not. I believe the scale goes from one to five. This particular ride, as I mentioned, had been secured by MPLLF using his Lyft account.

Not too long after his tirade, the driver pulled up to the circular drive at the JW Marriott and stopped to let us out. I was a bit surprised he didn't try to push us out. As we exited the car and started walking the 15 or so yards to the hotel's main entrance, MPLLF looked down at his phone and said to me, "Nice work, that guy just gave me a one-star rating."

Oops, sorry about that MPLLF. But other than that bad rating for MPLLF, it was another enjoyable evening in the insurance industry. Plus, he can just take regular cabs for a while, that's not such an inconvenience (to me!)

CHAPTER 37: THERE IS NO CHAPTER 37

The publisher (probably wisely, in the author's opinion) decided to delete one story that was not in keeping with the publisher's general guidelines of good taste and decorum. However, if you'd like to hear that story, which is hilarious (in the author's decidedly biased opinion), you can ask the author or his friend Jim Riely to tell you the story if you should encounter either of them in person. The story will not be recounted via email, text or in any other written form. Thanks for your understanding.

EDITOR'S NOTE: We always strive to help authors be their bests selves and in this instance, we couldn't publish the story (actually there were two of them that I deleted, but don't tell Larry) in good taste. Don't ask, because I'm not going to tell.

FINAL THOUGHTS

As mentioned previously, I feel that dedicating this book to the memory of Ryan Pincus will be another way of helping to keep his memory alive in the face of his tragic and untimely passing.

Ryan's death was a shock to all who knew and loved him. He was taken from us far, far too soon. The German philosopher Bertolt Brecht said, *"Do not fear death so much, but rather the inadequate life."*

Ryan's life was far too short, but it was certainly not inadequate. He brightened the lives of all who knew him. If this book can help to keep Ryan's memory alive in any way, no matter how small, then it will have been well worth the effort.

And, finally, while this book is dedicated to the memory of Ryan Pincus, I'd also like to mention the names of some other Professional Lines Insurance professionals who have left us far too soon (this list excludes those who passed on September 11, 2001; I have mentioned them in previous books).

Despite their absence, the memories of these people will long endure for those who knew them. They are:

John Bayeux

Paul Bertolotti

Bill Brown

Bill Cotter (the father)

Ray DeCarlo

Frank Englert

Ken Fekete

Joe Fine

Thomas Gamble

Richard George

Steven Gladstone

Perry Granof

Amy Brenneman Hodge

Bill Hopkins

Constantine "Dinos" Iordanou

Pat Jordan

Shaun Kelly

Elaine Tran Lenahan

Jim Magura

Toby Merrill

Mike Nikolai

Carole Lynn Proferes

Scott Shaffer

Barbara Seymour

Ron Swiner

Tom Vietor

Jon Vlachos

I'm sure I inadvertently omitted some worthy names from the list above. My apologies to the families of those people.

And please accept my sincere thanks, again, for your purchase of this book which, I hope, will help attract at least a few young people into our great industry. And, again, if you're interested in making a donation to the Ryan Pincus Memorial Fund, you can find it at: https://charitysmith.org/ryan-pincus-memorial-fund/

I leave you with this thought from English author Mary Ann Evans (who wrote under the pen name George Eliot):

"Our dead are never dead to us until we have forgotten them."

Ryan, smiling and happy, as we all remember him.

ABOUT THE AUTHOR

Lazarus "Larry" Goanos, a graduate of Red Bank (NJ) Catholic High School, Villanova University and Boston College Law School, has been involved with Professional Lines Insurance since 1989. He was an insurance attorney at law firms in New York City and Boston, before moving into senior positions with companies such as AIG, Marsh, ACE, Houston Casualty and Amwins. Since 2010, he has been the CEO (and President, CFO, General Counsel and janitor) of Andros Risk Services, an independent insurance consulting firm.

Larry is also the author of these insurance classics, available on Amazon:

- Claims Made and Reported
- D&O 101: Understanding Directors and Officers Liability Insurance
- Professional Liability Insurance: An Oral History

He may be reached at lgoanos@androsriskservices.com.